NEVER KNEEL DOWN

Never Kneel Down

Drought, Development and Liberation in Eritrea

James Firebrace with Stuart Holland
Preface by Neil Kinnock

 THE RED SEA PRESS
Publishers & Distributors of Third World Books
556 Bellevue Avenue
Trenton, New Jersey 08618   (609) 392-7370

First American edition 1985

THE RED SEA PRESS,
556 Bellevue Avenue
Trenton, N.J. 08608

Not for sale in Europe

ISBN 0-932415-00-8 cloth
ISBN 0-932415-01-6 paper

Cover photo: Mike Goldwater/NETWORK
Printed by the Russell Press Ltd., Nottingham

Contents

Preface

In Eritrea hundreds of thousands of children, women and men have been killed or crippled or turned into refugees in a war which began almost a quarter of a century ago.

Many more have died in the years of continual drought. Over a third of the population is facing famine.

As the people of Eritrea face another arid year and as the fighting intensifies Stuart Holland, the Labour Spokesperson on Overseas Development and Co-operation and James Firebrace, War on Want's Programme Office for the Horn of Africa, present an assessment of the successes of the Eritrean People's Liberation Front and make a plea for a much greater international appreciation of the educational, health care and other achievements made in spite of poverty and war by the EPLF administration. Its social and economic initiatives, they believe, can help to eradicate mass starvation. Basing their account on evidence gathered during their visit to Eritrea, Holland and Firebrace also urge that there should be an immediate and massive increase in all forms of emergency assistance to the Eritrean Relief Association. Without such help it is certain that many thousands more will die.

Never Kneel Down is set in the context of support for the people's struggle for self-determination. The authors argue that there can be no solution to the massive problems confronted daily by the people without an end to the war — and that will only come about when self-determination is secured.

I welcome the timely publication of this report and the opportunity it provides for Labour's approach, set out two years ago in our Programme for Britain, to be re-stated.

In that document we pledged support for self-determination for the people of Eritrea.

We promised financial and material help by the next Labour Government for the Eritrean People's Liberation Front and the Eritrean Relief Association.

We gave our backing to the proposal of the EPLF that there should be an internationally supervised referendum on the future of Eritrea — a referendum which would allow the Eritrean people to choose between full independence from Ethiopia, federal association with Ethiopia or regional autonomy within Ethiopia.

Nothing has happened since 1982 to make us change our view. Indeed, events since then have borne out our approach.

The tragedy of Eritrea provokes the sympathy of all who have seen the evidence of mass starvation and the results of conflict in television reports. But sympathy alone is not enough. Whilst we urge relief we must also get at the roots of the agony. There is a major responsibility on all of us to do whatever we can to help achieve a satisfactory settlement to stop the war — a settlement that serves the interests of both the Eritrean and Ethiopian peoples.

Earlier this year the European Parliament urged the Ethiopian Government to find a 'peaceful and negotiated solution of the conflict between it and the Eritrean peoples, which takes account of their identity, as recognised by the United Nations resolution of December 2 1950 and is consistent with the basic principles of the OAU'. That is a guide to action for other Parliaments and for Governments who can promote self-determination, stability and an end to the suffering of Eritrea and Ethiopia. And that most particularly includes the superpowers, both of which have, at various times, backed the Ethiopian Government, both of which are engaged in strategic competition in the area, both of which should be as ready with the means of giving life as they have been with the means of sustaining conflict.

In the meantime this book, by giving the facts behind the famine, provides an invaluable report of the situation on the ground as seen by two highly respected eye-witnesses, and it offers an invaluable insight into the issues. It will do a great deal to promote wider understanding of and support for the EPLF's case, and the recommendations listed at the end will arouse a much needed debate.

I commend this book to all who are genuinely concerned for the people of the region. But it should also command the attention of those many others — including our own Government — who have claimed to care about famine and conflict in the Horn of Africa but have failed to follow sentiment with effective aid, assistance and action.

Neil Kinnock MP

Introduction

For ten years Ethiopia has been notorious in the West for one of the world's worst droughts. Haile Selassie, likewise one of the West's best known African leaders, fell in 1974 through his failure to cope with the drought crisis which at that time affected all the Sahel or sub-Saharan region in Africa.* But he also fell because in a rule of half a century he failed to transcend the feudal structure he inherited. Friend of the Western democracies, who failed to help when Mussolini was his foe, he failed in turn to meet the demands for self-governing democracy in his own country. In that drama both the Ogaden in the south and especially Eritrea in the north played a key role.

This book follows a visit by the authors to Eritrea in April 1984 on the initiative of Neil Kinnock, Leader of the British Labour Party and George Galloway, War on Want's General Secretary. We went for four main reasons: (1) to report on the famine in Eritrea and its relation to the drought and the war, and the effectiveness of relief aid being distributed by the Eritrean Relief Association (ERA); (2) to examine the social and economic policies of the Eritrean People's Liberation Front (EPLF), to assess how these affect the Eritrean population, in particular the poorest and most disadvantaged groups, and to assess the role currently being played by external development assistance; (3) to assess the strength and significance of the EPLF as a political force; and (4) to evaluate the case made by the EPLF for Eritrean self-determination. The 1982 Labour Party Conference decided to back the referendum proposal of the Eritrean People's Liberation Front and to give aid to the EPLF and to the Eritrean Relief Association (see Appendix 6a).

Our findings and recommendations concern both the British Labour Party on the means of implementing its commitment to support Eritrean self-determination and to provide financial and material support to the EPLF and ERA, and also voluntary and governmental agencies on the immediate action necessary to relieve the suffering of the Eritrean people.

The mission comprised Stuart Holland MP, Spokesman for

*The Sahel in this wider sense is to be distinguished from the Sahel province of Eritrea of the same name.

Overseas Aid and Development for the Labour Party, James Firebrace, Programme Officer at War on Want for the Sahel and Horn of Africa, and Jenny Holland of the New Socialist. This report, and its conclusions and recommendations, is largely based on the visit to Eritrea itself (16th to 26th April 1984). We were able to visit and evaluate the EPLF's activities inside Eritrea, the relief supply route from Port Sudan, and ERA's programme in Port Sudan for refugees and for the disabled. The report also draws on extensive discussions and correspondence with many people, including aid agency representatives who have travelled elsewhere in Eritrea and ERA and EPLF representatives. We are most grateful to them for their help and cooperation.

Many people have helped us in the writing of this book. Special thanks for their extensive comments and suggestions on the text are due to Trish Silkin, Richard Johnson, Gunther Schroder, Roger Briottet, Paul Kelemen, Martin Ferns and Martin Plaut. We also thank Bill Bourne, who painstakingly word-processed the various drafts at every available hour of day and night, and Tony Simpson of Spokesman for his help with the book's production. Any errors of substance are, of course, our own.

'Never Kneel Down' is a popular slogan of the Eritrean People's Liberation Front.

James Firebrace and Stuart Holland

MAP 1 ERITREA: IN THE HORN OF AFRICA

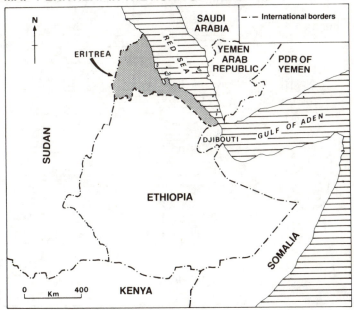

MAP 2 ERITREA: PROVINCES & TOWNS

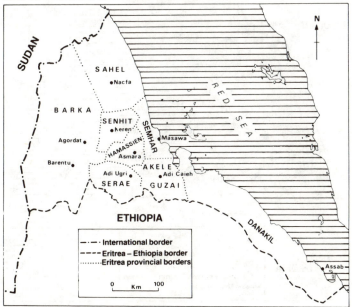

14

MAP 3 ERITREA: TOPOGRAPHY

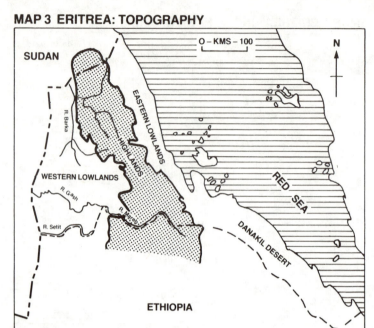

MAP 4 ERITREA: THE MILITARY SITUATION OF APRIL 1984

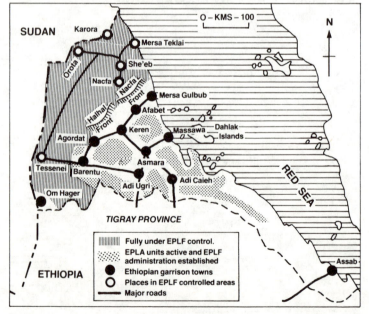

PART I

THE HISTORICAL AND POLITICAL CONTEXT

CHAPTER 1

The Eritrean Case for Self-Determination

For nearly a quarter of a century the Eritrean liberation fronts have fought a war against Ethiopian occupation. Their demand is for Eritrean independence. But successive Ethiopian regimes have claimed that Eritrea is rightfully Ethiopian and cite precedents dating back to the Queen of Sheba, whose liaison with King Solomon allegedly founded the dynasty of the 'Lion of Judah' in Ethiopia. How do such contrasting claims from the contemporary world and biblical myth compare in reality? Also, what role was played by Britain in the modern background of today's conflict?

In the 1940s the British occupation of Eritrea was faced with the question of Eritrea's future following its long colonisation by the Italians. Britain also was responsible for Eritrea's administration when the decision was made to federate Eritrea with Ethiopia in 1950, and therefore has a particular responsibility towards Eritrea. The eventual decision to federate Eritrea with Ethiopia reflected the strategic interests of Western powers, particularly the United States, and followed a period of violence sponsored by Ethiopia to intimidate those seeking independence for Eritrea. In the following decade the terms of the Federation were increasingly violated by Ethiopia, and culminated in Eritrea's formal annexation as the northernmost province of Ethiopia.

1.1 The Historical Background

Eritrea's history as a political entity dates from 1889, when the Italians occupied the area during the European scramble for African colonies. The Italians planned to transform Eritrea into a settler colony — taking the best agricultural land for farms and plantations, and later establishing a sizable manufacturing and light industrial sector. Roads, railways and ports were built to service the new shipping trade in the Red Sea following the opening of the Suez canal. But the large-scale build-up of the Italian population in Eritrea only started with Mussolini's war preparations against Ethiopia. By the 1940s Eritrea had an Italian population of 60,000 and had reached a relatively advanced stage of industrialisation, with about one in five Eritreans living in towns. The Italians directly controlled central political power, only allowing the traditional local leaders the authority to settle local disputes. When local positions became vacant, the Italians either secured the election or simply appointed a former soldier of their army or someone who had been working in their administration. But, as elsewhere in Africa, the common experience of foreign rule laid the ground for the development of a distinct national identity in Eritrea which was to become the basis for future demands for nationhood.

British Reforms...

With substantial assistance from the Eritrean population, the British army defeated the Italians in Eritrea during the Second World War and Eritrea was first controlled by a British military administration from 1941 to 1949, and then administered by the British Foreign Office until 1952. During the war years Britain built up Eritrean industry — and with it Eritrea's skilled working class of the Italian colonial period — to help meet the needs of a war economy.

After the war Eritrea suffered an industrial slump. Combined with increased local taxation, the resulting large scale unemployment contributed to a growth in the political consciousness of Eritrea's now considerable urban working class. In this postwar period the British removed or sold an estimated £86 million worth of industrial plant and equipment, including port facilities at Massawa and Assab, factories producing cement, potash, and salt, and railway equipment. (E.S. Pankhurst 1952).

During the British Labour administration of 1945-1951, some far-reaching political reforms were introduced, albeit principally to develop an Eritrean educated class as a political counterweight to the Italian settlers. Labour removed the official 'colour bar' of the Italian period, allowed Eritreans to participate in the administration, and promoted the formation of both political parties and trade unions. Not least, the Labour government also sponsored an extensive literacy and education programme.

...and Failures

After the war, the Peace Treaty with Italy provided that the future of her former colonies should be decided by the four major victorious powers — Britain, France, the United States and the Soviet Union. British policy, elaborated in the Bevin-Sforza plan of 1949, recommended partition — seeking to give the predominantly Muslim western Eritrea to Sudan and hand the Christian southern highlands to Ethiopia, even though this was unacceptable to all the Eritrean political parties. When the four powers failed to agree, a United Nations Commission, consisting of representatives of Norway, Burma, South Africa, Guatemala and Pakistan, was sent to Eritrea for two months in early 1950 to prepare a report for the UN General Assembly.

British administrators supervise the dismantling and removal of an Eritrean cement works in 1947 (source: E.S. Pankhurst, 'Eritrea on the Eve', 1952).

The UN Commission were to consider 'the wishes and welfare of the inhabitants of Eritrea... the capacity of the people for self-government ... the interests of peace and security in East Africa, (and) ... the rights and claims of Ethiopia, including in particular Ethiopia's legitimate need for adequate access to the sea' (see Appendix 1). But in fact the UN Commission's terms of reference were interpreted to suit the United States. The US Secretary of State, John Foster Dulles, put this succinctly in 1952:

> 'From the point of view of justice, the opinions of the Eritrean people must receive consideration. Nevertheless the strategic interest of the United States in the Red Sea basin and considerations of security and world peace make it necessary that the country has to be linked with our ally, Ethiopia.' (Quoted in Permanent Peoples Tribunal 1980).

The Commission also stressed the interests of Ethiopia by stating her need for 'legitimate' sea access which implied Ethiopian sovereignty over Eritrea. Its fact-finding and consultation was superficial. An observer wrote:

> '(The Commission did) no more than to carry out casual observations of rival political gatherings at each centre and address random questions to persons whose representative qualities it had no means of checking.' (Trevaskis 1960).

Meanwhile, Ethiopia intervened directly in Eritrea itself. The

leadership of the Unionist Party, which favoured union with
Ethiopia, was under Ethiopian direction; the Ethiopian Orthodox
Church added religious pressure by declaring that those supporting
independence would not be baptised, married, buried or receive
communion; and Ethiopia sponsored and armed a campaign of terror
and assassination against supporters of the 'Independence Bloc'. This
fomenting of internal unrest, which reached its climax immediately
before the arrival of the UN Commission, proved an important factor
in deciding the future of Eritrea. Some responsibility for this must
be borne by the British government, whose officials did little to
restrain Ethiopia in her attempts to prejudice the issue.

The UN Commission was split over its recommendations. Burma,
Norway and South Africa argued for close association with Ethiopia
on the grounds that Eritrea was poor and economically unviable and
that the majority of Eritreans favoured union. Guatemala and
Pakistan recommended full independence on the grounds that the
Muslim population would never acquiesce to union, and that an
independent Eritrea could decide itself at a later date whether or not
to federate with Ethiopia. The UN General Assembly of December
1950 accepted the majority position and recommended that Eritrea
become an autonomous unit 'with its own legislative, executive and
judicial powers in the field of domestic affairs', but 'federated with
Ethiopia under the sovereignty of the Ethiopian crown' (see
Appendix 1).

Federation and Annexation

In 1952 the new constitution for Eritrea was approved by its elected
parliament and the Federation came into being. The incompatibility
between a relatively democratic Eritrea and a feudal and autocratic
Ethiopia quickly became apparent as Ethiopia began to violate and
undermine the federal arrangement. Eritrean political parties and
trade unions, recognised by the Federal Act, were banned by the
Emperor who also expropriated the agreed Eritrean share of customs
and excise duty. The Eritrean Prime Minister resigned in 1955 in
protest against this intervention in Eritrean affairs.

In 1956 Tigrinya and Arabic, the official languages under the
Eritrean constitution, were suppressed and replaced by Amharic, the
offical language of Ethiopia, as the language of Eritrean official
communication and instruction. Strikes and demonstrations were
broken up violently by the police. Many people were killed during
a general strike in 1958 when police fired on a large demonstration
in Asmara objecting to the replacement of the Eritrean flag by that
of Ethiopia. Eritrean newspapers were censored. Industries were
closed and some factories (textiles, tanning and earthenware) were
transferred to Addis Ababa, a move which served both to weaken

Eritrea's economic base and to undermine the organised Eritrean working class as a political force.

The UN commissioner who drew up the Eritrean constitution in 1952 had stipulated that 'if the Federal Act were violated the General Assembly would be seized of the matter' (Final Report of the UN Commissioner). But although repeated missions were sent to the UN to demand its intervention, the stipulation was ignored. The Eritrean Liberation Front (ELF) was formed in 1961, arguing that the only remaining path to Eritrean independence was through armed resistance.

In 1961, elections were held for the third Eritrean parliament, but under strict Ethiopian control and without the independent electoral commission stipulated by the Eritrean constitution. This parliament finally 'accepted' the dissolution of the Federal arrangement and annexation of Eritrea by Ethiopia in November 1962. Controversy surrounds this decision. It is not even clear that parliament ever voted for annexation; one report (Tekie Fessehatzioni, 1984) states that the motion to dissolve the Federation was defeated four times, so that finally a declaration of annexation was merely read out. Certainly bribery, arrests and intimidation of members of parliament immediately preceded the event. Armed police were present in the chamber at the time, while the outside of parliament was cordoned off by military units. (Bereket Habte Selassie 1980).

In a confidential memorandum to the US State Department, now revealed through use of the US Freedom of Information Act, the American consul in Asmara, Richard Johnson, wrote:

> 'The 'unification' was prepared and perpetrated from above in maximum secrecy without the slightest public debate or discussion. The 'vote by acclamation' was a shoddy comedy, barely disguising the absense of support even on the part of the Government-picked Eritrean Assembly.' (Quoted in Tekie Fissehatzion, 1984).

After annexation the ELF's guerrilla activities increased and were met with harsh reprisals by the Ethiopians. By 1963 an estimated 3,000 Eritrean civilians were in prison on suspicion of sympathising with the ELF (Pool 1980). Villages were burnt and their inhabitants were either massacred or moved to sites which could be more easily controlled. In 1970, following an ELF ambush in which an Ethiopian general was killed, some 600 villagers were shot in nearby villages and the town of Keren was bombed with a reported 500 civilian casualties. 30,000 refugees fled from the area following the reprisals. In the towns arbitrary arrests, detention for long periods and the use of torture became increasingly common. In the early 1970s both the ELF and the Eritrean People's Liberation Front (EPLF), which had split from the ELF in 1970 (see Chapter 2) attracted many recruits from those who escaped from the towns.

As the war intensified, the Eritrean economy went further into decline. Eritrean factories were dismantled and moved to central Ethiopia. Much of Eritrea's skilled workforce either joined the liberation fronts or dispersed around the Middle East; many found jobs in Ethiopian towns far from the Eritrean conflict where new industry was booming because of the input of US capital. By the mid 1970s an estimated half million Eritreans were working in Ethiopia (Lefort 1981).

An Elusive Peace

The overthrow of Haile Selassie in 1974 and the radical reforms that characterised the first phase of the new regime in Addis Ababa brought fresh hope of a peaceful solution for Eritrea. Proposals were made in August 1974 for a return to a federal relationship by Aman Andom, nominal head of the Military Committee — the 'Derg' — which had seized power in Addis Ababa. But Andom was killed three months later on the orders of Mengistu Haile Mariam, who became the Derg's new Chairman. The atrocities in Eritrea and the attempts to crush the Eritrean liberation fronts continued. As the destruction of villages and crops and the arbitrary killings became more frequent, refugees again left Eritrea in large numbers. Amnesty International wrote of this period:

> 'During 1975-76 there were many other arrests of alleged opponents of the Government, including trade unionists, academics, senior officials in Government ministries, commercial and financial institutions, military officers, engineers, and state airline employees, teachers or students, some of whom had been in opposition to the previous government also... Eritreans continued to be a major target for political arrest, because of their suspected support for the armed struggle for the region's independence.
>
> Political detention in Eritrea, where martial law had been in force since 1970, followed the same pattern as under the former government, with large scale arbitrary arrests, torture and killings... Very few of these political prisoners have been tried, but none of them have been released from detention.' (Amnesty International, Human Rights Violations in Ethiopia, 1978).

In July 1975, the Guardian reported 30,000 refugees arriving in Sudan following a massacre at Om Hager in Western Eritrea. By the end of the decade 300,000 Eritreans were living in the Sudan as refugees and perhaps twice this number had been displaced within Eritrea.

In May 1976, the Derg put forward a 'Nine Point Peace Plan for the Eritrean Administrative Region' (see Appendix 3b), in which they proposed a political amnesty, assistance to enable the return of the refugees, and an 'exchange of views with the progressive groups and organisations in Eritrea'. The Derg sent a delegation to Asmara with

Housing conditions at Deim Kurea, Port Sudan where many refugees live.

orders to contact the EPLF. On the EPLF's insistence the delegation met with the ELF and the EPLF together. But the mission appears to have been little more than a cover for Mengistu to launch a hastily formed militia, 'the Peasants' Army', against both the Eritrean fronts. Ill-equipped and poorly trained, this army was routed after suffering massive casualties.

There have been numerous other attempts to mediate the conflict between Ethiopia and Eritrea. In March 1977 Fidel Castro came forward with a highly ambitious proposal for a federation between Ethiopia and Eritrea but including also Somalia and the Peoples' Democratic Republic of Yemen (PDRY). In late 1977, the Eastern bloc countries with East Germany as mediator brought the Derg and the Eritrean fronts together in East Berlin for a number of talks, which continued until June 1978 but came to nothing. In May the same year, the Soviet Union, Cuba and PDRY had brought back Negede Gobeze, a leading figure in ME'ISON*, from his exile in Paris to investigate the possibility of establishing an alternative government to Mengistu's based on the pro-Soviet wing of the Derg, the remnants of ME'ISON, the trade unions and possibly the Eritrean and other national movements. The attempt failed and led to the recall of the Cuban and South Yemeni ambassadors from Addis Ababa.

After a speech by Mengistu in June 1978 the Derg dropped any talk of 'progressive groups in Eritrea', and the EPLF and the ELF

*see Glossary.

were thenceforward lumped together as 'reactionaries' and 'Arab stooges'. When in November 1980 the EPLF put forward its proposals for an internationally supervised referendum to decide the future of Eritrea, the Ethiopian regime's only response was a new military offensive. In January 1982, Mengistu announced the 'Red Star Campaign' with a great fanfare of publicity. A vast military offensive to finally crush the EPLF, by then the only liberation front active inside Eritrea, would be combined with the reopening of factories and farms closed or abandoned during the war (Mengistu speech, Asmara, 25th January 1982). The EPLF held out against the offensive, tens of thousands of Ethiopian troops were killed and the economic plan never got much further than public rhetoric.

In the 34 years since the original UN decision on the postwar colonial future of Eritrea, many factors have changed. The Eritreans of today are very different from those trying to be heard in 1950. But the central issues are still the same. Eritrea saw European colonial rule disappear only to find herself once again under foreign domination after a limited period of partial self-government.

The British interregnum under the postwar Labour administration was positive in aiding social and economic reforms, but the unacceptability of the Bevin-Sforza plan opened the way to a contested UN 'solution' in the key question of relations with Ethiopia. US influence and backing for Haile Selassie until 1974 was followed by Soviet backing for the Derg in arms and aid thereafter. Cuban misgiving about the Derg's assault on the ELF and EPLF was real. But Cuban and East German diplomatic efforts to achieve a negotiated settlement have failed to secure Ethiopian agreement to the demand for Eritrean independence and self-government.

1.2 The Merits of the Eritrean and Ethiopian Cases

The EPLF's claims for the right to independence follow the same principle by which other African nations have defined themselves in post-colonial Africa. Basil Davidson wrote in 1980:

'If colonized African peoples have justly claimed and justly exercised the right to be free, and to build within colonial frontiers new nations of their own, resuming the development of their past history, then why should this right be denied to the Eritreans? They were colonized by the Italians, after all, in exactly the same way and in more or less exactly the same years as the rest of the continent was taken into colonial ownership and control. If they now find themselves formally within Ethiopia, that is not only a subsequent but also a similar development. Or if the colonial period proved to be, for other peoples, the 'forcing bed' from which there duly flowered the harvests of modern nationalism — the nationalism by means of which colonized peoples could throw off their subjection and stand upon their own — then why should it be denied that Eritreans, too, went through this same process, acquired a national consciousness during colonial rule, and came to feel the natural need for an assertion of their own identity? What today is so 'special' about the Eritrean case except that they happen to be colonized by an African, not a European, power?' (Preface to Sherman 1980).

Eritrea's separate political identity was forged during the period of European colonisation and this identity has not been lost over the subsequent years of Ethiopian occupation. On the contrary the budding nationalism of the 1950s has flowered under the brutality of Ethiopian military rule. The struggle waged by well-organised political forces able to act to defend Eritrean interests has provided a focus for this nationalism. Furthermore, in the areas now administered by the EPLF the population is once again experiencing different political structures and a different form of development from that of Ethiopia under Derg control.

Ethiopia's claim to Eritrea rests on its assertion that Eritrea has been part of 'Ethiopia' for 3,000 years. This is based on the fact that the ancient Axumite kingdom spanned both the current Tigray province of Ethiopia and southern Eritrea. After the fall of Axum there was a break of seven centuries before an influx of Abyssinians in the fifteenth century took control of much of present northern Ethiopia and the Eritrean plateau. As a recent historian comments: 'It is absurd to conceive of invasions and migrations of ethnic groups and tribes as a basis for the continuity of political control over a geographical area to justify rule over a people... History is always rewritten but usually without such good effect' (Pool, 1979). Ethiopia itself was created by Abyssinian expansion southwards and eastwards at the end of the nineteenth century — at the same time as Italian colonialism created Eritrea.

The historical arguments are important, but the crucial issue is that Eritrea was established as a distinct nation state through its more recent colonial history. Nowhere else in Africa have ancient claims been allowed to override the principle that the frontiers established by colonial rule define the new independent African states, with the exception of Morocco's occupation of Spanish Sahara (now Sahrawi Arab Democratic Republic), an act now opposed by a majority of the African regimes.

When the current Ethiopian military regime allied itself with the Soviet Union and the Eastern bloc, a new argument was brought in against the Eritrean case — that with a 'progressive' regime in Addis Ababa a liberation struggle was no longer justified. But a nation's right to self-determination does not change with a change in the occupying power. The Derg lost the possibility of a voluntary Eritrean union with Ethiopia when it continued Haile Selassie's policies of military suppression and the denial of elementary human and political rights. This, plus its failure to negotiate with the EPLF, calls into question its claims to be 'progressive'.

Eritrea's historical and political claims to self-determination are strong. But practical objections to its implementation may remain. We have seen how the UN decision for Federation was directed by Western interests. We now look at the three major practical issues that the UN Commission considered: (1) Ethiopian access to the sea, (2) the economic and political viability of an independent Eritrea, and (3) the interests of regional peace and security.

Access to the Sea

This is still a central issue. Ethiopian prosperity is indeed partially dependent on its overseas trade, but this is the case for other landlocked nations who must make customs and transit agreements with their neighbours. Much Ethiopian trade already makes use of the port of Djibouti. Economically, the additional cost to Ethiopia of using an independent Eritrea's ports would be insignificant compared to the sum now being spent on the war. Politically, the insecurity that Ethiopia might feel from lack of direct control over a seaboard is again minor compared to the insecurities that it and the region as a whole are suffering due to the conflict.

The EPLF has expressed itself ready to come to agreement on Ethiopian use of Eritrean ports provided that the Eritrean right to self-determination is recognised by Ethiopia (see Part III, Interview with EPLF Vice General Secretary). With the right political will, the issue of sea access can be resolved to the mutual advantage of both the Eritrean and Ethiopian populations.

Economic and Political Viability

In 1950 the delegates of the UN Commission who wished to deny Eritrea her independence argued against Eritrea's economic and political viability. Eritrea, they said, was a poor country, dependent on grain imports from Ethiopia and unable to form an independent government that would not disintegrate into anarchy and feuding. We have seen how the violence, fomented by Ethiopia during the period when Eritrea's future was being decided, helped create this impression. Whatever the situation was in 1950, the argument of non-viability would be difficult to sustain now. As we shall show in this report, we found that the economic potential of Eritrea is in fact considerable, and the EPLF has proved itself to be not only able to administer territory and provide health, education and other services to the population, but also to initiate fundamental political and economic reforms.

We discuss later the question of the unity and internal coherence of a future Eritrean government in a situation where fronts other than the EPLF are able to command some international support.

Eritrea is sometimes also said to be too small to justify independence — but a third of African states have an area less than Eritrea, and half of them have a smaller population (including Somalia and Libya).

Regional Peace and Security

The interests of peace and security in the region are clearly not served by the current situation, in which the war is causing the death and displacement of tens of thousands and is a major factor in the current famine. The Ethiopian government has argued that an independent Eritrea would be a threat to its security by potentially acting as a base for foreign invasion, particularly by 'Arabs'. The Derg has gone to some lengths to portray the Eritrean struggle as an Arab-inspired Islamic plot against Christian Ethiopia. However, the EPLF fighters and leadership include both Christians and Muslims and, while the EPLF has received some support from some Arab states, it has also been undermined by the more conservative states such as Saudi Arabia.

There is a further anxiety that allowing Eritrea to exercise its right to self-determination would set a dangerous precedent and give encouragement to opposition fronts among the constituent nations of the Ethiopian empire. Whatever the strength of the case of the national liberation fronts within Ethiopia, theirs is a different case from that of Eritrea with its distinct history of European colonisation. However, the intransigence of the Ethiopian regime towards the national question, both within its own borders and in relation to Eritrea, does strengthen the links between the Eritrean struggle and those of the nationalities within Ethiopia. It is this intransigence which is most likely to provoke the feared 'balkanisation' of the Ethiopian Empire. Peace and stability in the region will not be secured until the issue of democracy for the Ethiopian nationalities is resolved.

Elsewhere in Africa, governments are afraid that concessions to Eritrea will set off 'secessionist' demands within their own states. This is the concern of the Organisation of African Unity which in its founding charter 'determined to safeguard and consolidate... the sovereignty and territorial integrity of our states' (OAU 1963). This pronouncement should lead the OAU to review the status of Eritrea. The UN resolution of 1950 federating Eritrea with Ethiopia implictly, if inadequately, recognised Eritrea's separate identity and her territorial integrity distinct from that of her federal partner. The annulment of Eritrea's federal status in 1962, only a year before the founding of the OAU ran contrary to the UN decision and cannot form a legal basis for the recognition of a revised 'territorial integrity' for Ethiopia.

The OAU resolution of 1964 which calls for respect for the borders 'existing on the achievement of national independence' should support the case for Eritrean independence. Ethiopia can be said to have achieved her national independence either at the turn of the century when she successfully avoided colonisation by a European power or later in 1941 when she emerged from her 6 year occupation by the Italians. At both times Eritrea was treated as territorially distinct, but she has yet to be granted her independence.

After 23 years of warfare, in which hundreds of thousands have become refugees, and given famine conditions which are worsening year by year, the Eritrean conflict clearly calls for a radical change of strategy by the Ethiopian regime. It is important that the issue now be re-examined in the light of the basic principles of a nation's rights and the long term interests of the peoples of Ethiopia and Eritrea. Ending the war and ending the suffering are the humanitarian priorities. There seems to be only one way in which this will happen — to seek, and act on, the wishes of the Eritrean people themselves. This is also the path of international justice. In the next chapter we look at the social and political changes the EPLF is seeking to bring about in transforming Eritrea into a democratic and just society.

CHAPTER 2

The EPLF's Popular Revolution

The Derg claims that the Eritrean resistance is 'narrow nationalism'. It maintains that the Eritrean fronts give no consideration to internal social and political issues, or to the broader interests of the people of the region as a whole. This is distortion and propaganda, as mendacious in its way as some of the worst CIA propaganda on the Sandinistas in Nicaragua. In reality, the EPLF has prioritised the social transformation of a backward society, and gained mass popular support by its achievements which overshadow those of the Derg itself.

2.1 The Origins of the EPLF

The ELF emerged in 1961 as a liberal nationalist movement in reaction to the denial of political rights and repression by Haile Selassie's regime. The early ELF leadership was composed of former Eritrean soldiers in the Sudanese army, foreign-based intellectuals, and some nationalist politicians of the 1950s. Their social background and connections enabled them to attract substantial support from the upper strata of Muslim society in west and central Eritrea — tribal leaders, owners of large herds and merchants. Militarily the ELF lacked effective coordination, the Eritrean Liberation Army consisted of separate military sections under independent command.

The absence of proposals for much needed social change in the ELF's political programme, the lack of working structures within the ELF allowing fighters democratic participation in the decision-making process, the corruption of many leading ELF figures and their heavy-handed handling of national minorities such as the Kunama of the Gash region of Barka province, led to internal dissent and finally to divisions. Attempts to solve these internal problems were made at a series of meetings, including the ELF's Adobeha Conference of autumn 1969. The majority of the ELF leadership adopted a strong Arab and Muslim orientation and tended to be quite conservative in their social politics. Their younger critics espoused a secular Eritrean nationalism and radical policies for social transformation, while other critics of the ELF leadership differed on regionalistic grounds.

By the beginning of 1970, disagreements between the two groups reached a head. A large group of dissidents managed to escape the persecution initiated by the ELF leadership and reached the Danakil coastal area, where they formed in July 1970 the 'People's Liberation Forces 1'. Another group of dissidents established the 'People's Liberation Forces 2' in the eastern escarpment at about the same time. In February 1972 these two and a third group agreed to form a coalition and to gradually unite themselves into a single organisation. This process was achieved by late 1973 and the united forces took the name Eritrean People's Liberation Forces, which was renamed the Eritrean People's Liberation Front at their first Congress in 1977.

The early EPLF represented a coalition between the more educated eastern Muslims who initially formed the majority of the membership, and Christian highlanders. The EPLF leadership still reflects this original composition. The EPLF's programme of social transformation and their secular nationalism proved attractive to the younger generation of Christian students at high schools, colleges and university, who, after 1973, joined the EPLF in large numbers and now form the dominant element of the middle ranks. With the vast expansion in the EPLF in 1977 and again in 1980/81, its membership is now once again more balanced in terms of confessional, regional and ethnic composition.

The EPLF's stress on the need for social revolution to accompany military struggle, and its success in recruiting support, challenged the ELF, who in turn modified their own political programme. But this remained a largely paper exercise. It was the EPLF which began to implement its practical programmes for the social transformation of Eritrean society. By the late seventies, the EPLF had become the strongest front in Eritrea. In 1981, following fighting between the two groups (see Chapter 4), the EPLF drove the ELF fighters from their base area in Barka province into the Sudan.

The EPLF set themselves two tasks in the liberation struggle — to overthrow Ethiopian rule and to transform traditional Eritrean society. Both involve securing not only the support of working people and the poorest sections of the Eritrean peasantry but also their active participation in the struggle. Such participation is vital not only in the areas under full EPLF control and in the areas administered by the EPLF behind the front lines, but also in the towns nominally under Ethiopian control. In the latter areas giving practical support for the EPLF entails the possibility of reprisals, such as the massacre of an estimated 82 civilians by Ethiopian forces in Asmara on 12th September 1984 (reported in La Stampa, the Italian newspaper).

We describe here five aspects of the EPLF's political strategy — the creation of a political consciousness, the transference of local political power in favour of the poorer peasantry and of women, land reform, new roles and rights for women, and the structure of

EPLF decision-making. A sixth and central aspect — the military defence of the revolution — is described in the next section. In each of these aspects of its political strategy the EPLF seeks the involvement and participation of an organised population, at the same time leading it towards the goals of national unity, self-determination, and socialist transformation.

2.2 Creating a Political Consciousness

The EPLF's project for Eritrean society is based on a specific analysis of its respective classes and an assessment of their relationship to the liberation struggle. Unsurprisingly, opposition to the revolution comes from feudal landowners and those parts of the bourgeoisie prepared to cooperate with the Ethiopian regime. But the allies of the revolution are perceived as not only the poor and middle peasantry (including nomads), 'semi-workers' (who must take waged employment for part of the year) and the working class, but also most of the middle classes. The EPLF's strategy is to mobilise the bulk of the Eritrean population by carrying through reforms in their real and practical interest. Women are given a special emphasis in this process because of their additional exploitation in a still traditional society. The teaching of liberation for women forms a central element of the EPLF's political education, and over a third of its members are women.

A second issue stressed in political education is the unity and equal rights of the nine Eritrean nationalities and of Eritreans of different religious persuasions. This work is crucial if a future independent Eritrea is to avoid the divisions that characterise so many other states and if past differences are to be overcome. The EPLF are very conscious of this need and are putting considerable effort into generating a mutual respect between nationalities.

One EPLF leader told us that tackling the national and confessional questions within Eritrea was seen as being of equal priority to the women's question, with which it shares many of the same problems. Certainly the EPLF are trying to prevent the domination of political life by any one nationality. The EPLF Central Committee itself reflects a balance between the two main nationalities — Tigrinya (just over half of the Eritrean population) and Tigre (a third of the total), as well as between Christians and Muslims, who constitute about half of the population. Of the four members of the EPLF Standing Committee, two are Tigrinya and two are Tigre.

The issue of language is central. Primary education and adult literacy are now taught in the languages of four of the nationalities — Tigrinya, Tigre, Kunama and Afar. We saw textbooks in the different languages being produced on the presses of the Department of Information. A common language of communication is necessary

and Tigrinya — the language of around 50% of Eritreans — has
been given this status. The issue of a common script has yet to be
resolved: there are currently three scripts in use for different
languages — Ge'ez (the ancient script of the Ethiopian Coptic
Church), as well as Arabic and Latin. Unity between nationalities
and religions is fostered through dramatic shows in which dances

*Poster stressing the role to be played by Eritrea's nine nationalities
in the EPLF revolution.*

are performed in the national dress of all the nationalities, including especially the small minorities.

The EPLF broadcasts information on the radio in five languages, including Amharic, the official language of Ethiopia. Although Ethiopian troops are forbidden to listen to EPLF broadcasts, it is often the only way they can receive news of military and social developments in Eritrea. Military defeats are never reported on the official Ethiopian radio, and fictitious football results from Mersa Teklai were reported by the Ethiopians even after the rout of their army by the EPLF (of which we saw the transparent evidence on our visit). The EPLF, while also reticent about reporting military setbacks, make no attempt to stop Eritreans listening to the Ethiopian broadcasts, and many fighters in the base areas listen to Addis Ababa regularly.

The EPLF's political education aims to achieve a popular awareness of Eritrea's history, of the colonial past, of the background to the current conflict, and of the reasons for the EPLF's national struggle. The Information Department produces radio broadcasts, magazines and school textbooks on these themes. On our own visit we were struck not only by the morale and motivation of the people we met, but also by their detailed knowledge of the history of their struggle.

To carry out the work of political education and mobilisation at local level, the EPLF train 'cadres' who are selected from among the civilian population, giving priority to women, to members of the minority nationalities, and to people from recently liberated areas. Recruits are sent to cadre schools and many thousands have now received the training of two to three months. Cadres are taught about the situation in Eritrea and about the EPLF's policy, about struggles elsewhere in the Third World, and about the most effective way of organising the population. On their return to the community, cadres are expected to take a leading role in encouraging the formation and development of mass organisations and village committees, while otherwise resuming their normal lives.

2.3 People's Political Power

In attempting to transform Eritrean society the EPLF must balance two factors — the need to maintain the ideological and political direction of the revolution, while fulfilling the aspirations of the majority of the population and ensuring their commitment. The EPLF describe this process as a revolution 'from above and from below'.

From above, the EPLF has developed its own structures of overall administration and coordination. The cadres who have received EPLF training are seen as a 'vanguard' to mobilise the population and encourage development of the new structures of the Eritrean revolution. From below, the people are to elect their own local administrations according to the EPLF's principle of 'people's political power'.

The central problem the EPLF must confront is how to break the power of the landowners and feudal chiefs to whom the population has deferred in a highly hierarchical society. Where the EPLF's presence in an area is new, village elections are held after a period of political education by the front. The villagers nominate candidates and the whole village population openly elects a temporary 'People's Committee', which might include former office-holders of an ELF or Ethiopian administration.

From this beginning, the EPLF carries out detailed studies of the village population, which it classifies into 'social forces' — peasants (poor, middle and rich), women, youth, workers (in the towns), and 'professionals' (shopkeepers and artisans). The EPLF establishes its 'mass organisations' from these groupings. In areas firmly under EPLF control the villagers elect a 'People's Assembly' from the nominees of the mass associations. The number of elected representatives from each mass organisation is in proportion to the size of that 'social force', thus ensuring that poor peasants and women are well represented on the People's Assembly. This represents a fundamental change from the composition of traditional village assemblies where women and the landless were totally excluded.

The People's Assembly establishes committees with particular responsibilities: land distribution; livestock (controls on grazing); agriculture (collective fields, preparing terraces or water catchment schemes); economy (fixing prices, collecting taxes from markets, organising people's shops and cooperative workshops, road building); social affairs and health (women's rights, help for the needy, selection of health personnel, village sanitation); forestry and water development; settling local disputes; political education,education and culture; and security.

The EPLF establishes 'Resistance Committees', which it sees as an intermediate organisational form between People's Committees and People's Assemblies, in areas where the EPLF presence is not secure against Ethiopian incursions or where the ELF had a long history of undisputed control. The Resistance Committees are elected from the candidates of the EPLF mass organisations, which are set up clandestinely in these areas. Their task is to organise the village to prepare the ground for the eventual creation of a People's Assembly, to protect the village against enemy influence, and to eradicate any remaining political influence of the ELF.

People's Committees, Resistance Committees and People's

Assemblies are now operating at village level throughout the 85% of Eritrea where EPLF units and militia are active. According to EPLF statistics 582 people's administrations had been established by 1981, the majority in the more densely populated provinces to the south. These structures enable the EPLF to implement its programme of social transformation, while being able to be flexible if it feels unable to counter local resistance, whether caused by conservatism, cultural reasons or the impracticability of the change proposed. However, the current structures do place limitations on the future political plurality of Eritrea, and the EPLF will have to confront this issue when working through the implications at local level of its proposal for an Eritrean National Assembly (see Appendix 2b).

The EPLF mass organisations are the channel for civilian support for the EPLF. They are established separately for peasants, women, students, and workers, and are organised at a regional level within Eritrea and abroad, in the Middle East, Europe, and North America. Each of these mass organisations has its own central committee and holds its own congress. Mass organisations are also being established for 'youth' and 'professionals' but these are not yet organised at a national level. The role of the mass organisations is crucial in explaining the nature and objectives of the EPLF, in organising the population, and in ensuring their contribution to the EPLF's struggle. Within Eritrea they play an important role in economic and social life — by setting up 'people's shops' and 'people's pharmacies' and by establishing cooperatives and mutual aid teams.

The mass organisations of the Eritrean population living outside Eritrea play an important role in raising funds for the EPLF. Congresses of the European mass associations are held bi-annually in Bologna, and are attended regularly by several thousand Eritreans who listen to updates on the situation in Eritrea from Central Committee members, give reports on their own work in Europe and fix programmes of activities for the next two years. Congresses enable the Eritrean diaspora to keep in touch with other Eritreans and with developments in Eritrea.

2.4 The EPLF's Land Reform

Of the EPLF's various economic reforms, land redistribution is by far the most significant. Land is central to economic prosperity, and in many areas the injustice of land distribution, or of denial of access to land, had become burning issues of discontent.

Traditional land tenure in Eritrea before the Italian occupation was relatively egalitarian. Under the 'diesa' system, land was the common property of the village with every family head having equal right to its use. A redistribution occurred every seven years to take account of changing needs. But additionally some families owned private 'risti' land, which made them the richest farmers and gave them local political power.

In the colonial period, Italian settlers took over the best land in the highlands and large areas of low-lying land for large commercial farms growing cash crops. Supported by the Italians, the owners of 'risti' land were able to influence the communal 'diesa' system to their favour. The poorest peasants were forced to find work in the towns, or on the Italian-owned commercial farms. During the period of British rule, Italian settlers acquired further tracts of land and, with Federation, landowners and church officials who had supported unification with Ethiopia were rewarded with property. The effect was to polarise landholding in Eritrea — the poorest sectors of the peasantry led a tough, insecure and indebted existence, while absentee landlords lived comfortably in the towns from the produce and rents of their large holdings.

With the growth of Eritrean armed resistance to Ethiopian rule, the relationship of the liberation struggle to these social issues became increasingly important. In the mid 1970s the EPLF began an initial land reform in the highland areas where their units were active. The reform was based on the traditional 'diesa' system, which had lapsed so that in some areas no redistribution had taken place for 40 years. But important modifications were introduced: women were allowed to own land for the first time, absentee villagers were able to keep land only under certain strict conditions, and the charging of high rates of interest on loans to poor peasants was banned. Some land was put aside to be farmed collectively by the village, with the produce being used to help finance local services — the building of a clinic or school, payment for teachers and health workers, or buying anvils for workshops producing agricultural tools.

The EPLF describe their land reform as a carefully planned process carried out over a period of some months. EPLF units begin by calling meetings of the village population to discuss land problems and organise the most receptive peasants in small groups to carry out surveys of the situation of each family. Women are encouraged to participate in these groups. This organisation results in poor peasants and the landless, including women, being elected for the first time onto the village committees. Such a change in the balance of local power is a precondition for practical land redistribution. Because of the prior organisation through local group structures the peasantry are prepared to deal with opposition to the reforms, and violence and bloodshed are largely avoided. In Wadi Labca in 1976, for example, when the landowners organised demonstrations against the proposed reforms, they were met by larger counter-demonstrations.

EPLF statistics record that by 1981 land redistribution had been achieved in over 160 villages, resulting in nearly 50,000 families gaining additional land and 12,500 landless farmers acquiring plots for the first time. Clearly landowners and peasants with large holdings lost out in this process. In densely populated areas, land reform has led to the fragmentation of land into small parcels. In these situations the EPLF has encouraged a second stage land reform where larger plots are farmed by cooperatives and mutual aid groups. During the recent drought, such organisation has become important for poorer peasants who lack tools or must hire oxen for ploughing (Robinson and Wardle 1983).

The EPLF have generally distributed half of former state lands to the landless, while keeping back half for production to assist its own needs for food. Land redistribution continues in areas which have recently come under EPLF control. In July 1984, state land in the vicinity of Tessenei was distributed to over 1,000 formerly landless peasant men and women, many of whom had been living in ERA's displaced people's camps. In this case distribution involves writing out new leases and is unlikely to encounter resistance. In those parts of the former ELF areas where land reform would involve expropriation, the EPLF land reform has not yet begun as the process of laying the necessary political foundations has yet to be completed.

Following the overthrow of Haile Selassie, extensive land reform took place in Ethiopia, particularly in the southern Oromo areas. But little change occurred in the Ethiopian-administered areas of Eritrea until after the 'Red Star Campaign' of 1982, when every garrison was instructed to carry out land redistribution in the surrounding area. In areas where the EPLF had already carried out their own reforms, the Ethiopian 'land redistribution' resulted only in the confiscation of the produce of the village's communal land on the grounds that it was being used to support EPLF activities. Elsewhere, in areas near the towns, the EPLF say that Ethiopian attempts at land redistribution resulted in armed clashes within the village as the army had previously armed villagers including the larger landowners. The EPLF told us the case of Adi Tserai in Serae province where seven people were killed in such clashes in March 1984.

Among Eritrea's nomadic population, inequalities of wealth and local power are different from those within the settled population. A defined class structure already existed in the pre-colonial period. An aristocracy claimed tribute in the form of labour services or in kind from serfs. Unrest among the serfs grew during the colonial period, and the serfs' agitation led the British authorities to abolish all the obligations of serfdom. However, the aristocracy maintained their dominant position by virtue of their large herds and inherited status. The ELF, which received material and political support from these traditional lowland chiefs, made no attempt to redress the disparities of wealth in the nomadic population. The EPLF, which now controls these areas, is planning to resettle poor farmers from the overcrowded highlands into the Gash area where there is little shortage of land. However, such resettlement must be undertaken sensitively as this land is inhabited by the settled Kunama population, whose support the EPLF are keen to secure.

The EPLF has now started a detailed study, similar to its analysis of the land-holdings in settled communities, of the nomadic and semi-nomadic population according to size of herd. The EPLF's Programme (see Appendix 2a), which argues for the settlement of the nomadic population is giving way to a greater understanding of nomadic life and of nomads' contribution to the economy. Continued rethinking will be necessary if the EPLF is to avoid giving less consideration to the interests of the nomadic population than to the settled population, and therefore unequal treatment to different nationalities. The current drought has decimated Eritrea's herds and intensified the ecological damage caused by years of overgrazing. The priority must now be to limit the future size of the herds so that the capacity of the environment is not exceeded and the interests of those with small herds are protected.

2.5 New Roles and Rights for Women

The EPLF have recognised the particular oppression of women in Eritrea. They see women's emancipation and their full participation in social production and the political process as central to the success of the revolution. Women's rights occupy an important place in the nine points accorded to the issue in the EPLF's National Democratic Programme (see Appendix 2a). But, as was clear from our own experience and discussions with women in Eritrea, women's rights also have become part of the everyday struggle of the EPLF.

Traditionally in rural Eritrea, the role of both Christian and Muslim women in production was given secondary importance to that of men. Men's work - ploughing and herding — were seen as the central tasks of the agricultural and nomadic economy respectively. The roles that women play in the domestic sphere and in the settled population's agricultural production were accorded small significance. This downgrading of women's contribution to family welfare is expressed in an Eritrean proverb, which itself is echoed elsewhere throughout the Third World: 'Where is the gain if one marries a woman to give birth to a woman?' In fact the workload of Eritrean women is extremely arduous — they take full responsibility for all domestic chores — grinding grain, preparing food, gathering firewood, fetching water, looking after the children and cleaning the home. In the farming areas women also weed, harvest and grow vegetables.

Eritrea's relatively industrialised economy employed many women — but women were paid less than half the wages of men and were laid off when expecting a child. Women also worked as wage labourers on the settler plantations and as domestics to well-off urban families — in both cases for long hours at minimal wages.

Women were allowed no role in political life and were excluded from attending the discussions of village assemblies. They were not considered to hold opinions of any worth — one Eritrean proverb runs: 'Just as there is no donkey with horns, so there is no woman with brains.' Very few girls went to school, and in the mid 1970s, 95% of Eritrean women were illiterate. Women had minimal social rights — parents often arranged the marriages of 11 year old girls to much older men. A man could divorce his wife easily, but as a woman's return to her family home might involve her parents having to return the dowry, she would be unlikely to receive support from them if she wished to leave her husband.

Those women that were able to leave their husbands often had little choice but to earn a living as prostitutes. Early Italian settlers had taken Eritrean women as concubines, but prostitution emerged on a large scale in the 1930s when the Italian population in Eritrea rose from 5,000 to 50,000 with the influx of Italian soldiers and labourers employed to build roads before the planned invasion of Ethiopia. With the decline of Eritrean industry since Ethiopian postwar intervention in Eritrea, female employment became scarce and prostitution among Eritrean women again became widespread, particularly among young female refugees who had fled to Sudan.

The EPLF's land reform has been of major significance for women, who can now own land in their own right. This is self-evidently important for older divorced women who were previously vulnerable to extreme poverty. The EPLF's changes to the system of village elections mean that women now elect their own representatives at the People's Assembly. Women's mass organisations provide a forum where they can meet together separately from men and discuss the issues which concern them. The mass organisations also provide political education, literacy classes, and a broader involvement in the work of the EPLF. EPLF legislation also defends women's social rights. The 1978 marriage law outlaws child marriages and marriages arranged without the full consent of the couple concerned. Women have gained equal rights with men to divorce and to inherit.

But it is within the ranks of the EPLF and among EPLF cadres that the most marked changes in women's roles and in attitudes to women have taken place. Political education has had a powerful influence, but the exigencies of a guerrilla war also make a nonsense

30% of the EPLF are women with roles which include front line combat and skilled work in the workshops of the base area.

of any sexual division in labour. Women make up 30% of the EPLF and over 15% of the combatants. These proportions are increasing with every new intake of recruits to the EPLF. As we saw at first hand, women are active organisers, teachers and administrators, as well as mechanics, electricians, electronic engineers, watch repairers, tailors, barefoot doctors and village health workers. No women were elected onto the EPLF Central Committee at the last Congress in 1977 — EPLF leaders claim that to have done so would have been tokenism, for at that time no woman had had a long experience of the EPLF struggle. But changes are expected at the next Congress as there are now several potential candidates.

Bringing about similar changes in women's role is taking longer in civilian society than in the front itself and is meeting varying degrees of resistance, particularly in areas where the EPLF presence is relatively new or is necessarily transient. The war and the needs of the struggle are an important factor in pushing for the increased participation of women, just as they have been in other wars in Europe and elsewhere. The current commitment cannot guarantee women's emancipation in a future Eritrea, but the legislation already introduced and the structures which ensure women's political representation are only likely to be reversed or dismantled with difficulty.

2.6 The EPLF's Organisational Structure

The EPLF began fifteen years ago as a handful of guerrilla fighters. It now has a complex and sophisticated structure. This is shown not only in the People's Assemblies and the mass organisations already described. It also is shown in the revolution's decision-making 'from above' — where the military strategy of the Eritrean People's Liberation Army (EPLA) and the policy of the EPLF Departments is determined.

The organisational structure of the EPLF has evolved over the past decade, but the basic structure was formalised during the National Congress of 1977. This adopted the constitution of the EPLF, endorsed the National Democratic Programme (see Appendix 2a), and elected the 37 members of the EPLF's Central Committee. The 1977 Congress was attended by 900 delegates from the EPLA and the mass organisations, some 11% of whom were women. (This and much of the other information in this section derives from correspondence with G. Schroder, researcher into recent Eritrean history). Congresses should be held every two years, but the EPLF say that the continuing military pressure of several major Derg offensives has meant that a second full Congress has had to be delayed. Recent announcements indicate that preparations for the Second Congress are now being made.

The Organisational Structure of the EPLF

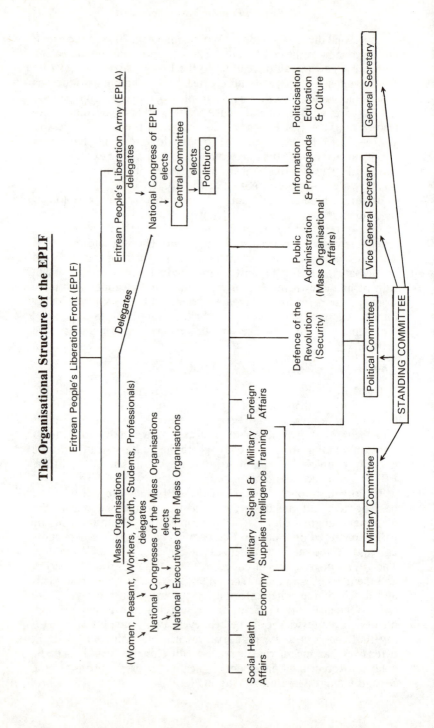

In broad terms the EPLF consists of the Eritrean People's Liberation Army, which forms the bulk of the armed forces, and the mass organisations, which represent the civilian wing of the EPLF even though they too contribute to the armed forces through the people's militias. The EPLA is organised into brigades and each member of the EPLA is assigned to a brigade. In practice, many 'fighters' serve in the 'non-military' departments carrying out technical and administrative work, but if necessary they can be integrated back into the brigades at short notice.

The Central Committee of the EPLF elects from among its members the General Secretary and the Vice General Secretary and the other eleven members of the Politburo. Each of the latter heads one of eleven Departments — somewhat akin to Ministries in the more usual governmental context. The larger Departments, particularly those of Economy and Political Education and Culture, are divided into numerous sections. Decisions of the EPLF are made by the Central Committee; between sessions of the Central Committee by the Politburo; and between sessions of the Politburo by the 'Standing Committee' consisting of the General Secretary, the Vice General Secretary, and the heads of two groupings of Department heads — the 'Political Committee' and the 'Military Committee'. The Standing Committee takes the day-to-day decisions of the organisation on both military and political matters.

The Politburo appoints the administration for the zones, each of which includes at least one Central Committee member. The elected village administrations relate to these EPLF zonal committees. The Department of Public Administration (formerly the Department of Mass Organisational Affairs) is crucial for the success of the revolution, for if mistakes are made by this Department then the vital relationship between the EPLF and the population may be put at risk.

We met several of the EPLF leadership. It is difficult not to be struck by their relative youth. Most Central Committee members are in their thirties. They also were both unassuming and accessible. We frequently only learnt some time after a meeting that an individual held a senior position. In spite of their youth all the leadership have experience as fighters — in some cases as long as 20 years. Because of this common experience the EPLF leadership forms a relatively homogeneous group, which to date has been largely free from the factionalism that has characterised the Derg and the ELF.

It is clear that the EPLF have devised a political strategy which has gained the support of the Eritrean population — in spite of the resistance of traditional power structures and the competing pull of the Ethiopian authorities who have sought to develop their own administrative structures — the 'kebeles' and the peasant associations. In defining the path of the revolution, the EPLF have assessed the measures that will enhance both the economic welfare of the more oppressed sections of Eritrean society and the degree of control they exercise over the decisions affecting their lives. But the EPLF has not simply reflected the demands of the people. Some reforms, such as the granting of land to the landless and the incorporation of women representatives into the People's Assemblies, have met with quite extensive opposition.

In this sense the revolution is very much two way — from above as well as from below. It also depends upon internal and external forces. In the next chapter we look at the role played by outside powers in the Eritrean conflict.

CHAPTER 3

Eritrea versus the Superpowers

From its beginning, the Eritrean struggle has had an international dimension. In spite of the changes in international alliances in the region, foreign powers have consistently armed successive Ethiopian regimes against Eritrea, and have frustrated the hopes for a negotiated solution.

3.1 The US and its Allies

Intervention by the United States in Eritrea dates from before the UN resolution of 1950, when the US government indicated that once Ethiopia gained sovereignty over Eritrea the US would seek to take over the large British communications centre outside Asmara, the Eritrean capital. This was the basis for US support for the union of Eritrea with Ethiopia. In 1953, shortly after Federation, the US obtained use of the centre, which they named the Kagnew Station, in return for military aid to the Ethiopian government.

Kagnew became the largest intelligence gathering centre outside the US, staffed by 3,500 American personnel. In many years, US support to the Ethiopian armed forces made up two thirds of US military aid to the whole African continent. Much of the training and equipment that the US provided was used against the ELF and in particular was used to established a crack unit — the 'commandos' — which received training from the Israelis in anti-guerrilla warfare. During the period up to 1974 Ethiopia was also a major beneficiary of US economic aid.

Since the Derg took power in 1974, US assistance to Ethiopia has dried up. In 1976 the US government pressured USAID and the World Bank to reject Ethiopian requests for aid, and since 1978 the US has been concentrating its aid to the region on Sudan, Somalia and Kenya. US policy for many years was to wait and see how the relationship with the Soviet Union would develop. In 1980 the US handbook for Ethiopia noted:

'(Analysts dispute) the depth and permanence of the commitment of Mengistu and his colleagues to the Soviet variety of Marxism-Leninism as opposed to their commitment to the retention of power and to central control of political life, the economy and society. According to some observers, the long-range stability of the relationship between Ethiopia and the Soviet Union was uncertain... At issue was whether that

Captured ammunition boxes. The Ethiopian army was armed first by the USA and then by the Soviet Union.

adherence would persist if the regime's dependence on Moscow for survival diminished or if the Soviet perspective on a matter of immediate relevance to Ethiopia's interests ever differed from that of Mengistu.' (Ethiopia, a Country Study, 1980).

The US is now seeking actively to woo Ethiopia back into its sphere of influence. Secretary of State George Shultz met the Ethiopian Foreign Minister in October 1983 to 'iron out differences', and discussions are under way regarding compensation for American firms whose assets in Ethiopia were nationalised after the revolution. The World Bank resumed aid in 1980 and gave $40 million per annum in 1980-84 (African Economic Digest, Special Report, Sept. 1984). On the Eritrean question, the US has consistently denied support to the movements for national self-determination, even for those groups who have opposed the socialism of the EPLF. For the US the goal is still to win back an Ethiopia complete with the occupied coastal province.

British foreign policy has coat-tailed that of the US. In July 1984 Malcolm Rifkind, Minister of State for African Affairs in the Foreign and Commonwealth Office, made the first official visit to Ethiopia since the revolution, and the British ambassador in Addis is pressing for a substantial aid programme. At the same time some MPs on the right wing of the Conservative Party are calling, on the basis of crude anti-Soviet policies, for British foreign policy to ally itself with Somalia and with the case for Eritrean independence, through support for the ELF-PLF, a small Eritrean front with no presence inside Eritrea but diplomatically active in London and in the Middle East. The only likely effect of such moves will be to create confusion about the true nature of the struggle being waged in Eritrea. By contrast, the British Labour Party has for some time supported Eritrea's right to self-determination and its programme now commits it to support the EPLF referendum proposals and to commit aid to the EPLF when in government (see Appendix 6a).

The European Economic Community has differed from the US on developments within Ethiopia. The European Development Fund replaced the US as the main source of international assistance to Ethiopia, which is now the largest single recipient of EEC aid in Africa. Recently the EEC has begun to recognise the need to complement this aid with assistance to the sizable areas of Ethiopia outside governmental control and has therefore begun to make grants to the Eritrean Relief Association. On the political side, the Confederation of Socialist Parties of the European Community are sympathetic to the Eritrean position (see Appendix 5c), and the European Parliament as a whole resolved in April 1984:

'to strongly urge the Ethiopian government to find a peaceful and negotiated solution of the conflict between it and the Eritrean peoples which takes account of their identity, as recognised by the United Nations resolution of 2 December 1950, and is consistent with the basic principles of the OAU' (see Appendix 5b).

This resolution is an indication of the growing impatience among Western supporters of Ethiopia with its pursuit of a military solution in Eritrea.

3.2 The Soviet Union and its Allies

The Soviet Union's position on Eritrea has gone through a complete about-turn. The Soviet delegate to the UN in 1950 said:

> 'The USSR has consistently supported the proposal that Eritrea should be granted independence and has continued to do so at the current session. We base our argument on the fact that all peoples have a right to self-determination and national independence... The UN must take a decision which will satisfy the longing of the Eritrean people for independence and freedom from national aggression. The General Assembly cannot tolerate a deal by the colonial powers at the expense of the population of Eritrea.' (Appendix 1 of Selassie 1980).

Furthermore, the Soviet Union played a role in building up the ELF, albeit through third parties, in the 1960s and early 1970s. In 1977, during the Ogaden war, the Soviet Union made its dramatic switch of alliances, withdrawing its support for Siad Barre's 'socialist' Somalia, abandoning its naval base at Berbera and throwing its full weight behind the Derg by organising a massive airlift of arms to Addis Ababa. At the end of the Ogaden conflict, Soviet military hardware was moved north and played a decisive role in driving the Eritrean fronts back from their almost complete control of Eritrea.

In 1984, the Soviet Union has 3,000 military advisers in Ethiopia. It has also built a naval base in the Dahlak islands off the Eritrean coast, and has equipped an Ethiopian army (now estimated to number 300,000) with some 1,000 tanks, 1,500 armoured cars and 90 Mig planes and helicopter gunships. Three quarters of this military aid is on a loan basis, and Ethiopia is estimated to have run up a military debt of between $2,000 million and $5,000 million. (Africa Economic Digest, Special Report September 1984). The Soviet Union justified its reversal of position on Eritrea by declaring that the Eritreans were now 'objectively helping the realisation of imperialist designs' and that 'the genuine interests of the population (of Eritrea) coincide with the interests of the entire Ethiopian people, which is trying to build a life on new principles.' (Pravda 1978 quoted in Selassie 1980).

The Ethiopian determination to impose a military solution on Eritrea has proved a particular embarrassment for both the Cubans and the East Germans. Cuba was training Eritrean fighters in the late 1960s, and in 1974 tried to put the Eritrean issue on the agenda of the Non-Aligned Conference in Havana. Both Cuba and East Germany were still giving political support to the EPLF in late 1976. But in December 1977 Cuba sent troops to the Ogaden to help the Ethiopian army push back the Somalis. East Germany began training Ethiopian security services. Since 1979, the Cubans have made a point on a number of occasions of stating that their troops are not fighting in Eritrea, even though in practice they strengthen the overall Ethiopian military position by relieving the pressure on its army in the Ogaden. In July 1984 Cuba announced that it was reducing its troop levels as a result of 'the Ethiopian armed forces' increased strength in combat capacity.' (Summary of World Broadcasts ME/7688/ii, 6 July 1984).

3.3 Arabs and Africans

The Arab countries are described by the Derg as the initiators and backers of the Eritrean fronts — in fact the truth is much more complex. The ELF during its active period (1961-81) often portrayed the Eritrean struggle as Islamic, which helped attract support from some conservative States. Of more significance was Arab concern over Ethiopia's alliance with Israel. Over the years the fronts secured Arab support from countries with as varied political philosophies as Egypt, Algeria, Sudan, Iraq, Syria, United Arab Emirates, Kuwait, Libya, Yemen Arab Republic, the People's Democratic Republic of Yemen (PDRY), and Saudi Arabia.

However, the Soviet Union's switching of its support to Ethiopia led Syria and the PDRY to stop their support for the fronts. The PDRY had provided the EPLF with port facilities for its boats, but in 1977 sent a mechanised division to Eritrea in support of the beleaguered Ethiopian army. Libya withdrew support to the fronts in 1981 on signing a tripartite mutual defence pact with PDRY and Ethiopia. Sudan's attitude to the Eritrean fronts is dependent on the state of her complex relationship with Ethiopia. Sudan and Ethiopia mistrust each other, and Ethiopia supports Sudanese opposition movements in order to pressurise the Sudanese government to cut its support for the Eritrean fronts and to limit their movement in Sudan. Generally the Sudan has backed the non-EPLF fronts, but has tolerated the EPLF presence and the transit of goods to Eritrea through Sudanese territory.

Saudi Arabia is wary of the EPLF which it sees as both Christian and socialist. Saudi Arabia gives support to the various remnants of the ELF and to the ELF-PLF. These fronts came to a Saudi-sponsored unity agreement in Jeddah in January 1983. The Saudis' action seems intended to prolong the conflict in order to weaken a hostile Ethiopia. It appears that the EPLF now receives its material and humanitarian support in the Middle East from only Somalia, Kuwait and the United Arab Emirates.

Many black African states are sympathetic to the Eritrean case but have proved reticent in lending their united support to Eritrea. As we have noted, the Ethiopian definition of the Eritrean fronts as 'secessionist' and the fear this raises for those states' own internal cohesion has been a powerful factor in ensuring their silence. Furthermore, Ethiopia has particular prestige within Africa — it successfully resisted colonisation by a European power, and Addis Ababa is the seat of the OAU. Nevertheless, Mozambique, Guinea-Bissau, and Madagascar have at various times sought to mediate in the Eritrean conflict. The Sahrawi front, Polisario, once more vocal, now keeps silent because it needs Ethiopia's support for it own battles within the OAU. Other African States, dependent on one or other superpower, are reluctant to speak out.

Successive interventions of the superpowers have denied the Eritreans military victory, while local political factors in Africa and the Middle East have limited the international political support the EPLF is able to mobilise. Such support can only come from governments able to pursue a foreign policy independent of both the US and the USSR and which are also distant from the immediate repercussions of the conflict. In Europe, the EPLF's natural allies are socialist parties, the labour movement, and the peace movement as Europe attempts to distance itself from the cold war politics of the US. The European Community may prove to be a powerful advocate for a peaceful settlement to the extent that political pressures from the Strasbourg Assembly are effective.

CHAPTER 4

The Military Development of the Eritrean Struggle

The Ethiopian government refers to the EPLF as 'bandits' and refuses to acknowledge that they pose anything more than a 'security problem'. In fact the EPLF is now able to field a well-trained army whose size is estimated by informed observers to be between 40,000 and 50,000 men and women. The EPLF has captured and can now mobilise some 150 tanks and armoured vehicles, as well as heavy and light artillery, rocket launchers and anti-aircraft guns. The EPLA is now a larger and better equipped army than those of most African states, and is approaching in size the armies of Ethiopia's larger neighbours, Sudan and Somalia.

The EPLF's military strategy is shaped by four considerations. First, it has always had primarily to depend on Ethiopia as a source of arms: weaponry must be captured, mostly in battle but also in guerrilla raids on specific targets.

Second, the EPLF has to face a much larger military force, several times its size (two-thirds of the Ethiopian army is stationed in Eritrea), and with sophisticated up-to-date equipment. The EPLF

EPLF artillery in the NE Sahel coastal plains, March 1984.

EPLF fighters in the coastal plains, April 1984.

has to compensate for this disadvantage by better trained and more committed fighters. It must also avoid engaging in battle and defending positions where Ethiopian control of the air is decisive, and it must make maximum use of surprise attacks.

Third, the EPLF needs to be able to repair and maintain its military equipment, feed its army and care for the war wounded. It does this, as we have seen on our visit, by defending a mountainous base area which is secure from enemy ground attack and within which it has developed a complex series of underground workshops and garages, its own production farms and camouflaged hospitals.

Finally, the EPLF must secure popular support during a protracted war. It has done so not only by carrying through reforms but also by defending the population through the 'people's militias', responsible to the village assembly, and 'zonal militias', responsible to the EPLF Regional Command. It also avoids putting the civilian population at risk. One implication is that the EPLF see little advantage in capturing and then holding the towns although they have the military capacity to do so, because the Ethiopians would simply bomb the towns from the air. Bombing raids have already largely flattened the two sizable towns held by the EPLF — Tessenei and Nacfa — causing extensive loss of life and property and an exodus of refugees.

4.1 The First Phase

There have been two main phases in the military development of the Eritrean war. A first phase from 1961 to 1977 saw the expansion of the fronts from guerrilla bands to substantial well-armed armies. In the first decade, attacks by ELF guerrillas were answered by Ethiopian reprisals, often directed against any civilian population suspected of lending them assistance. In these reprisals Ethiopian forces burned villages, sometimes massacring hundreds of villagers. Waves of refugees began to pour into Sudan — 60,000 after the first major Ethiopian offensive against the ELF in 1967, and 100,000 following a second offensive in 1970. As a result the sympathy that might once have existed among some sectors of the population for a close relationship with Ethiopia rapidly disappeared.

The period 1970 to 1974, when the ELF and the newly-emerged EPLF fought a civil war, is a bleak period in Eritrea's history. This ended when the revolution in Ethiopia made it imperative for the fronts to hold a common position to confront any proposals that might come from Addis. By this time the EPLF was establishing itself as a powerful force. During 1974/75 it further strengthened itself by successfully recruiting Eritreans with military training from the Ethiopian police force in Eritrea, and from the Eritrean commando units which it had successfully defeated. A large influx of young people joined the EPLF after 56 students were garotted with electric cable in Asmara in January 1975.

By mid 1976, with the launching of the 'Peasant Army' offensive against Eritrea, it was clear to the fronts that the Derg's 'Nine Point Peace Plan' (see Appendix 3b) had been intended merely to buy time and to reopen the divisions between them. The EPLF laid seige to Nacfa in September 1976. The town finally fell six months later, an event followed by a series of EPLF victories. Between March and July 1977 the EPLF took Karora, Afabet, Elaberet, Keren and Decamhare. It also surrounded Asmara, Eritrea's capital, leaving it accessible only by air, and organised the escape of 800 political prisoners from Asmara's jail. The ELF took Tessenei in March, Agordat in August, Mendefera in October and laid seige to Barentu. In October 1977, the fragile peace between the two fronts was shored up by a unity agreement in Khartoum. By the end of the year, mainland Massawa was in the hands of the EPLF, which now had captured tanks and armoured vehicles. This was to mark the limit of the advance of the first phase.

4.2 The Second Phase

The second phase of the Eritrean war began when the Soviet Union intervened in December 1977. The Soviet navy, by shelling EPLF positions from their battleships, prevented the EPLF from taking the port section of Massawa. A massive airlift of Soviet tanks and other arms allowed the Ethiopian army to push back the Somali forces in the Ogaden, and by May/June 1978 these troops and heavy armour were available for redeployment in Eritrea. In two offensives in June and November 1978, the Ethiopian army retook most of the towns held by the Eritrean fronts.

For the EPLF the return to the northern base areas was 'a strategic withdrawal'. Certainly it minimised civilian and military casualties. It also allowed the EPLF to give battle at strategic points of its choosing, to evacuate towns and to remove plant and equipment to its base area. Only the evacuation of Keren appears to have been a last-minute affair when the landing of Ethiopian troops on the northern coast forced the EPLF's Standing Committee to reverse its previous decision to defend Keren. However, the EPLF claims not to have lost a single engagement during this period and to have captured further arms. For the ELF the story was different — in attempting to hold territory its casualties were high. The balance of military power between the fronts had now shifted strongly towards the EPLF.

Recognising its weaker position, the ELF began in 1979 to respond to Soviet proposals transmitted through the PDRY, where it still held an office. In return for its agreement to autonomy within Ethiopia the ELF was offered the reins of government in Eritrea. Fighting again broke out between the ELF and the EPLF and in early 1981, following ELF attacks on its positions, the EPLF responded with a three month offensive against the ELF base area in Barka. The ELF's military defeat was total. ELF fighters either changed sides or fled to Sudan, and the EPLF became the single front with a military presence in Eritrea. EPLF administration was established in the ELF areas and consolidated in the areas from which the fronts had withdrawn during the retreat but in which EPLF guerrilla units had continued to operate.

In early 1982 the EPLF successfully resisted the largest offensive the Ethiopians have ever mounted in Eritrea. This 'sixth offensive' or 'Red Star Campaign' was advised by Soviet military experts and involved 15 divisions totalling over 100,000 troops and a new range of weaponry including helicopter gunships. But the EPLF was well prepared and had weakened the force of the offensive by surprise attacks in the preceding months. Its lines held and the morale and confidence of the EPLF were given a massive boost. The Ethiopian army had received a severe setback with estimates of their killed and wounded varying between 37,000 and 43,000. A seventh offensive by the demoralised Ethiopian army, launched this time without publicity during the first half of 1983, succeeded in breaking the Halhal front at some weak points. But within four months the EPLF had regained all its former positions, and the offensive ended having made no headway. Its net effect was to strengthen the range of military equipment at the EPLF's disposal.

4.3 A New Phase?

After the military stalemate of the last five years, the Eritrean war seems in 1984 to be entering a third phase with the EPLF moving onto the offensive. The EPLF's capture of the town of Tessenei and of the important farming area around Ali Gidir in January 1984 indicate the extent to which it has mechanised its army. This was the first time it had won tank battles in open plains. Two months later, using tanks and armoured vehicles supplemented by those captured at Tessenei, the EPLF won what is undoubtedly the single

Captured Soviet tanks were deployed by the EPLF during the fighting on the NE Sahel front, March 1984.

EPLF record 3122 Ethiopian prisoners of war taken during the fighting on the NE Sahel front.

most significant battle of the war to date. EPLF fighters with mechanised armour pushed through the North East Sahel front, and in a classic 'pincer' movement over a 100km front destroyed an Ethiopian armoured division, deployed in the area with supporting tank and artillery battalions.

In the first battle on 22nd February, the EPLF broke through the first line of trenches and reached the coastal plains. In the second and larger attack between the 19th and 21st of March, the EPLF overran all the remaining Ethiopian positions in the area, including the Ethiopian headquarters at Awget, the airstrip at Mahimimet and the small port and supply depot at Mersa Teklai. The EPLF say they took 3,122 prisoners in these battles and estimate that 5,000 Ethiopian troops were killed and that some 300 escaped to Sudan, while the rest fled south overland or were evacuated by sea.

Visitors who arrived in Eritrea within days of the battle include Uschi Eid, a member of the West German Parliament, who saw the prisoners of war and some of the captured military equipment being taken inland, and Egil Hagen, an aid official who had formerly been on a number of UN peacekeeping assignments as a major in the Norwegian army. Hagen stressed that he was impressed by the evidence of the battle. Coming to Eritrea with an image of the EPLF as sandal-shod guerrillas, he found that they had mobilised at brigade level and won a classic World War II type tank battle. Initially sceptical of EPLF claims, he told us that, having seen the scale of the fighting that had taken place, he judged EPLF claims on

Ethiopian soldiers surrender to an EPLF fighter, Mersa Teklai, March 1984.

casualties to be broadly accurate. We visited the battle sites in April 1984, a month after the EPLF's entry, and saw the remains of destroyed tanks and trucks, a range of empty barracks and supply depots, and bodies of Ethiopian soldiers missed over the vast battlefield by the EPLF units burying the dead.

Against Ethiopian denials that EEC food aid is being distributed to troops, in Mersa Teklai on the coast we were shown boxes of butter-oil marked 'Food aid of the European Economic Community to the People of Ethiopia'. EPLF fighters now guarding the area told us they had found these in the Ethiopian army stores and in their trenches.

The North East Sahel victory is significant for two reasons. It has broken a third of the encirclement of the EPLF's Sahel base area, leaving lines of confronting trenches only on the Nacfa and Halhal fronts (see Map 4). It has allowed the EPLF to capture the fuel and ammunition it needs to make good use of its captured armour, as well as its artillery and anti-aircraft guns. A few days before our arrival in Eritrea, the EPLF shot down a Mig-23 fighter plane, one of many shot down in the last two years.

The Sahel victory was followed in May by another remarkable success when an EPLF commando raid on the Ethiopian airforce base at Asmara used rocket launchers and hand grenades to destroy or damage severely a large number of military planes. Independent sources in Ethiopia have now confirmed that ten planes were destroyed and over twenty damaged. This represents about a fifth of the entire Ethiopian air force.

The evidence of the first six months of 1984 indicates strongly that the military balance is moving towards the EPLF. The EPLF arsenal now includes tanks and armoured vehicles which it can maintain and repair itself and which it has already put to good effect in two major battles. While the focus of the war in the near future is likely to be guerrilla operations against roads and garrison towns in the densely populated highlands, the EPLF has the capacity to fight conventional pitched battles when it chooses to do so.

Mengistu's visit to Moscow in March 1984 and the visit of the Soviet Union's Deputy Minister of Defence, Marshal Petrov, to Massawa in July indicates that the Ethiopians are likely to acquire yet more sophisticated armaments in an effort to keep ahead of the EPLF. But will this reverse the current EPLF advantage?

In terms of morale the EPLF has a strong advantage. As a result of recent victories, the morale of its fighters was extremely high at the time of our visit. The Ethiopian army on the other hand has suffered humiliating defeats and heavy casualties. The Ethiopian authorities go to great lengths to hide defeats from the army and from the civilian population — including the already cited reports referring to football matches by the Tessenei and Mersa Teklai teams broadcast after the garrisons had been overrun. It is reported that Ethiopian officers are arrested after a defeat and the EPLF claim that desertions of officers are increasing. Furthermore, many of the Ethiopian troops are young conscripts recruited against their will, and fighting a war they do not understand.

The most serious evidence of dissent occurred in October 1982 when the Ethiopian army in Eritrea had to put down a mutiny within its elite Third Division. A number of brigades made demands ranging from requests for leave to return home to see their families to calls for a public explanation of the fate of the Red Star Campaign. The two brigades which marched to Asmara to present their complaints were attacked by other sections of the army and the dissenters either killed or arrested.

4.4 The Human and Material Costs of the War

In the longer term, the drain of the war on Ethiopia's economy and human resources will be critical. The Derg has to pay for nearly three quarters of Soviet military aid, and expenditure has consequently soared. Ethiopian spending on defence and internal security rose from 14% of total government spending in 1970 to 21% in 1976 and was estimated at over 30% in 1979 (Ethiopia, a Country Study 1980). In 1983/84 defence and security take up 45% of Ethiopia's total budget for capital expenditure of $598 million. Meanwhile World Bank estimates put per capita GNP at $140, one of the lowest in the world. (Africa Economic Digest Special Report, September 1984).

Compulsory conscription was introduced in 1983 and the Ethiopian army grew to more than 300,000 in 1984. (The Military Balance 1984-1985 gives a figure of 306,000 for the size of the Ethiopian armed forces.) This force, comparable with the armies of major European powers, represents a massive drain on Ethiopian manpower resources. In the agricultural sector drafting into the army has contributed to the current food shortages and famine.

It is likely that over 100,000 Ethiopian troops have been killed in Eritrea in the last seven years alone. The EPLF claim to hold 7,500 prisoners of war and we saw thousands of them in the northern base area. Most of these are Oromos from southern Ethiopia. We interviewed some of these prisoners, who include high-ranking Ethiopian officers. They confirmed that they are well treated by the EPLF. They are fed and provided with adequate water, and given

The EPLF estimate 5000 Ethiopian troops killed during the fighting on the NE Sahel front — the most significant EPLF victory of the war to date.

medical care and shelter. All of this is as yet without assistance from the International Committee of the Red Cross. The existence of such a large number of prisoners of war, whose existence is denied by Ethiopia, and who receive no support from the Red Cross is an international scandal.

Within Ethiopia the growing numbers of prisoners will create increasing political problems for the Derg. They are international proof of the defeats the Ethiopian army has suffered and they are potential recruits for Ethiopia's national opposition movements, particularly the Oromo Liberation Front which is becoming increasingly active in the south of Ethiopia.

The EPLF has to date released a large number of prisoners — the largest group of 3,000 was released in October 1981. Many of those freed decided to stay in Eritrea, fearing accusations of desertion if they returned to Ethiopia. We met a group of them who were earning a living on construction projects in the EPLF base area, while farming their own small vegetable plots.

In the short and medium term a military victory is impossible for either side — for the Derg because the Ethiopian army is tired, demoralised, beset by internal dissent and has little heart for the fight; for the EPLF because if they capture towns they will be bombed to rubble. But the EPLF, on the evidence to date, are likely to consolidate and increase their military strength as the war continues. The Derg uses Soviet support to continue its only strategy — the escalation of the war with yet more troops, more fire power, and more losses. The devastating human and economic cost in one of the poorest, most famine-ridden countries in the world should be self-evident.

CHAPTER 5

Prospects for the Future in Eritrea

Past reporting on the Eritrean conflict is replete with failed predictions. In 1977, when the fronts controlled practically the whole of Eritrea, outside observers claimed that Eritrean independence was imminent. In 1978 as Ethiopian forces newly backed by the Soviets retook town after town, and in 1982 as the preparations for the massive sixth offensive got under way, the impending defeat of the Eritrean resistance was confidently asserted. Past experience as well as an examination of the current balance of military factors indicate that there will be no outright military victory for either side in the near future.

So what will influence the outcome of the Eritrean conflict? In May 1976 the Ethiopian military regime declared its 'Nine Point Peace Proposal for the Administrative Region of Eritrea' (see Appendix 3b) in which they recognised the right to self-determination of all nationalities as defined by the Ethiopian National Democratic Programme, declared the resolution of the Eritrean conflict as a priority, and proposed discussions with 'progressive groups' in Eritrea. But a few months later the Derg launched its Peasants' Army into Eritrea and since that time it has never publicly countenanced anything but the military destruction of the Eritrean opposition. Of the two adversaries, this leaves only the EPLF with a proposal that could halt the fighting.

The EPLF's 'Referendum Proposal' of November 1980 (see Appendix 2c) proposes a ceasefire to be followed by an internationally supervised referendum to allow the Eritrean people to choose between (1) national independence, (2) federation or (3) regional autonomy. During the period preceding such a referendum all parties — whether EPLF, other Eritrean groups, or the Ethiopian government — would be free to canvas among the people for the support of their respective positions.

The present situation must give the EPLF a diplomatic advantage. It has publicly shifted from an outright demand for independence to insisting that the Eritrean people decide their own future. The Derg on the other hand has moved only in the direction of increased militarism. Proposals for an eventual limited autonomy for the nationalities (but not to Eritrea as a distinct entity) have been made at the first Congress of the Workers' Party of Ethiopia in September

1984. It remains to be seen whether any practical developments emerge from this or whether the proposals prove, as in the past, only to have been the rhetoric of an important political occasion.

The EPLF's position is strengthened by its declaration that when granted its basic demand for self-determination, it will negotiate access for Ethiopia to Eritrea's ports. However, the EPLF sticks adamantly to a position of future non-alignment, in which it would allow no foreign bases on Eritrean soil or in Eritrean waters. Such sentiments will be applauded by those governments concerned about the global military build-up of the superpowers.

There is little doubt that in the event of a referendum the Eritrean people would opt for independence. In the first place, after a generation of war with the Ethiopian regime, they could hardly wish for an association in which responsibility for defence and security remains with Addis. Secondly, Ethiopian massacres of civilians are still being reported. The EPLF has evidence of the slaughter of 36 civilians in Naro district in April 1984 and of 42 villagers killed when the Ethiopian air force bombed Mulki in Serae province in early October. Finally, in the rural areas at least, the EPLF enjoys wide popular support.

Since the 1978 retreat, the urban population has had only clandestine contact with the EPLF and one can only speculate on the current extent of its support. If the reaction to the liberation of towns in 1977 is indicative, this support will be considerable. Two factors are significant. First, there is the likely influence of relatives who have joined the front and, second, the reaction to militarisation of the towns which are now accommodating large garrisons of Ethiopian troops and where security is restrictive or repressive. Eritreans leaving the towns are giving reports which indicate a political apathy, with the Derg's administration at community level — the kebeles — acting as little more than recruiting agents and fundraisers for the Ethiopian war effort, and as a security apparatus to detect EPLF sympathisers. Significantly, six months after the EPLF's liberation of Tessenei, eyewitnesses have reported that a third of the original population has now returned.

Among the refugees there are many who had fled Eritrea before the emergence of the EPLF and who had sympathised with the ELF. Support for the ELF has dwindled since the front lost its capacity to influence events in the field and disintegrated into factions. Nevertheless, the refugees, particularly those in Sudan and the Middle East, do represent the only significant source of Eritrean support for these ELF factions. Although there is little doubt that the refugees would opt for an independence which would guarantee them a livelihood and security in their home country, a united position between the fronts will be an important factor in their future

Father brings his daughter, wounded during an aerial bombardment, for treatment at the EPLF's Zara Hospital.

mobilisation.

As we have already seen, relations between the ELF and EPLF have had a long and difficult history. But unity would make it easier to win outside support and recognition, and, after independence, to avoid the kind of internal conflict currently being faced by Angola and Zimbabwe. In October 1982, the EPLF proposed the formation of a national coalition of the different fronts into a single national army which would then pool its resources and pursue a unified military strategy (see Appendix 2b). In March 1984 the EPLF successfully came to agreement with the ELF-CC (the 'Beten group') — one of the smaller groupings — and has allowed its 1,000 fighters to return to Eritrea from Sudan.

The EPLF proposals include a call for the fronts to form an Eritrean National Assembly which would prefigure the government at independence. The existence of such an Eritrean 'provisional government' would simplify the raising of the Eritrean issue at such international fora as the UN and the OAU. However, the other splinter groups — the ELF factions and Osman Sabbe's ELF-PLF — have rejected the terms of the EPLF's military and political proposals. One disadvantage of the unification proposals for these groups is that they they would then no longer have independent use of the funds they now attract from different Arab regimes. With this income they are able to keep up extensive contact with the international media and with national governments, and are able to exaggerrate their own importance in the Eritrean struggle, such as by claiming to have a military presence inside Eritrea.

Internal developments in Ethiopia itself will be central to how and when the Eritrean conflict is resolved. There are three factors — the role of the opposition fronts within Ethiopia, the effect of demoralisation and frustration within the Ethiopian armed forces, and the attitudes of the outside powers on whom the present regime depends.

All the opposition fronts in Ethiopia recognise the Eritrean right to self-determination and independence. The EPLF support the aspirations to self-determination of the nationalities within the Ethiopian empire, and recognise that a lasting peaceful solution to the Eritrean conflict depends on the democratic resolution of the national question in Ethiopia. Some of the fronts in Ethiopia have themselves acquired considerable arms, have widespread support from the local population and administer large areas of the country. This is particularly true of the Tigray People's Liberation Front (TPLF) which operates throughout the northernmost Tigray province immediately to the south of Eritrea.

The weakness of the opposition in Ethiopia stems from the lack of a single agreed political programme through which pressure can be exerted on the Derg. The TPLF have called for a 'United Democratic Front' of progressive groups, but of the main groups the Western Somali Liberation Front (WSLF), the Oromo Liberation Front (OLF) the TPLF and the Ethiopian People's Democratic Movement (EPDM)*, only the latter two have reached agreement. With differences over the geographical extent of the respective national domains and over final objectives, the development of a single programme and a unified opposition is likely to take time.

Demoralisation and dissent within the Ethiopian military will grow as the Eritrean war continues. If the EPLF continue to score dramatic victories, the demand from military units in the field for a peaceful solution will become more vociferous. The task of the Derg's proliferating intelligence network within the army, set up to identify and neutralise dissent, will become increasingly difficult. An army divided within itself is unlikely to fight effectively.

But the central determining factor will remain the actions of outside powers. The current Ethiopian regime is totally dependent on the military support of the Soviet Union without which they cannot pursue the war. This is reflected in Ethiopia's public stance. The Soviet Union has been putting pressure on the Derg to form a party for a number of years. This is now happening and the Workers' Party of Ethiopia was launched on the 10th anniversary of the Ethiopian revolution, in September 1984. This party is the creation of the Derg, formed to further its own interests, and to accommodate its global sponsor. Party members are carefully screened and the Party leadership takes over the government of the country from the Derg. But nine of the eleven Executive Committee posts of the Party are filled by the military members of the Derg's own standing committee, and Mengistu is the Party Chairman.

Reciprocally, the Soviet Union is also tied to the policies of the Derg. While an ongoing war guarantees Soviet indispensability to the Derg, Soviet strategic interests can only be met with Eritrea controlled by an accommodating regime. The Soviet Union will be more determined than ever not to lose their facilities in Eritrea now that they have heavily invested in the development of a naval base on the Dahlak islands just off the Eritrean mainland.

In spite of the military and political bonds with the Soviet Union, Ethiopia's economic links are with the West. Trade with the Comecon countries accounts for less than 10% of the total, and Eastern Bloc project financing is only $30 million a year. Ethiopia is the single largest recipient of EEC aid, receiving $110 million under the current European Development Fund allocation. Ethiopia will also receive between $300 million and $400 million from the World

*see Glossary.

Bank in 1984 and 1985, and has secured substantial aid agreements
with Italy, France and Federal Germany. The US and Britain have
frozen aid until compensation to companies nationalised by the Derg
has been finalised. In spite of the political upheavals of the last
decade, Ethiopia has recovered as a popular trading partner for the
West:

> 'Opportunities may be limited, but business is avidly fought for — not
> only because of the recession but also because Ethiopia always pays its
> bills. This first class repayments record applies not only to commercial
> transactions, but also to Ethiopia's non-military debt... Such
> conservative management, which has included tight controls over the
> money supply and a seven year wage freeze, has induced some countries
> to take an attitude to commercial relations diametrically opposed to
> their aid positions.' (Africa Economic Digest April 1983).

In one of the many ironies of the Horn, the Soviet Union's military
support is protecting the profitable investment and trade of the West.
East and West thus jointly deny Eritrea its basic rights and allow
the war and the suffering to continue. And in the unlikely situation
of the US drawing Ethiopia back into its fold, there would be little
change for Eritrea.

The recent resolution of the European Parliament — to urge the
Ethiopian government to negotiate a peaceful solution to the Eritrean
conflict which takes account of Eritrea's identity — is significant.
By virtue of its aid relationship, the EEC has political weight in
Ethiopia. It remains to be seen whether progressive forces in Europe
and the Third World can carry such initiatives in the wider
international arena. If so, combined with the pressure of an escalated
armed struggle in Eritrea, this could prove to be the elusive key to
Eritrean self-determination.

PART II

A NEW MODEL
FOR DEVELOPMENT

Introduction

For those with experience of Third World countries the following scenario is only too familiar. An industrial or mineral investment project surveyed and scrutinised by skilled personnel proves to be inappropriate in size and scale to real development needs. The project is controlled and supervised by foreign management and local managers shadow their foreign counterparts, dependent on them for know-how and access to information and spares, without which the plant cannot operate.

In drought areas in Africa it also is typical for there to be major transport problems. These arise not only from the very long distances, frequently in tropical or desert conditions, but also from the absence of the skills and equipment needed to run modern transport networks. For instance, one of us visited Chad, Niger, Mali and Upper Volta ten years ago at the time of the Sahelian famine. It was common in Chad at that time either to find that the heavy lorries for drought relief had been abandoned through over-use without adequate servicing, plain misuse or inability to undertake repairs or get spare parts. Attrition rates were high, and the average anticipated lifetime of a heavy truck was little more than a year.

In contrast with such production and distribution problems encountered in many Third World countries, the Eritrean People's Liberation Front clearly has (1) produced a range of sophisticated goods with its own skilled labour; (2) achieved a repairs service with a reliability which would be envied in several developed countries; (3) machined spare parts ranging from crank shafts and cylinders through to reprocessed tyres; and (4) produced capital goods and equipment such as presses or medical equipment at a high level of sophistication on the simple copy and substitute principle. How has it managed so well and achieved so much with so little external assistance?

CHAPTER 6

Self-Reliance in Production and Distribution

During the debates of the British colonial era, before the UN decision of 1950, one of the arguments used against the case for Eritrean independence was that Eritrea was economically unviable. Eritrea's economy had been distorted to support the war efforts of first Italy, prior to her invasion of Ethiopia in 1935, and then Britain in the latter years of the Second World War. This was one reason why the country's administration and public services were subsidised by Italian and British grants.

6.1 Eritrea's Industrial Past

The peasant farming sector of Eritrea was abysmally poor and still is, but even by the late 1930s Eritrea had a commercial farming sector exporting cotton, coffee, sisal and tropical fruits and a substantial light industrial sector with a large skilled labour force.

Although the British sold off and dismantled much machinery and equipment — thereby serving to justify their argument against independence — Eritrea still had a greater industrial capacity in the 1950s than the whole of the Ethiopian empire which, with ten times the population, was hampered by archaic feudal structures. By the standards of other African colonies of the period, industry in Eritrea was highly developed. In 1939, there were over 846 registered transport companies, 624 construction works, 2,198 trade companies and 728 light industrial concerns. With their development, Eritrea had generated a highly skilled and extensive working class. In 1952 there were several electricity power stations, printing presses and tanning firms. Eritrean industries were producing chemicals, soap, canned meat, dairy products, edible oil, bread, pasta, canned sardines, beer, wines, brandy, mineral water, soft drinks, bricks, tiles, lime, marble, cigarettes, matches, batteries, nails, wire, tyres and paper.

During the federal period from 1952 to 1962, Eritrea's large skilled labour force and easy accessibility from the sea continued to offer a profitable area for foreign investment. The large Barattolo cotton factory dates from this period, as well as the commercial plantations and tomato canning plant at Elaberet. Haile Selassie's ban on trade unions further attracted foreign capital. The Emperor's own efforts, backed by large sums of US capital, concentrated on developing

Ethiopia's industrial capacity in the central Shoa province at the heart of the empire. But by 1970 Eritrea still accounted for over a third of the industrial activity of Ethiopia and Eritrea combined.

The upsurge in fighting in the mid 1970s between the new regime in Ethiopia and the liberation fronts severely disrupted Eritrean industrial production. The Derg dismantled and transported whole factories to Addis Ababa and thousands of workers fled at the time of the government's Red Terror campaign either as refugees or to join the fronts. By the end of 1977 the fronts controlled all of Eritrea except Asmara and two other towns, but were unable to operate most of the factories for lack of raw materials and missing or damaged parts. In spite of the difficulties, the EPLF were able to operate the power stations in all the towns they occupied, maintain telephone communications and water supplies, and run some smaller factories including the Keren groundnut and incense processing plants.

The EPLF made maximum use of the period 1977-78 to expand their light industries in the base area, bringing out machinery and raw materials from the towns they captured. Thousands of skilled and semi-skilled workers joined the EPLF to be employed in the workshops of Sahel province and in operating the newly acquired plant and equipment. Most of the workers we met on our trip had joined the front at this time. The EPLF estimate that in 1977 alone the number of skilled workers in the EPLF increased threefold; by the end of the year they were producing millions of pounds worth of material and covering 80% of the needs of the front.

Since the withdrawal of the fronts to their base areas in mid 1978 the EPLF's industrial sector has continued to expand, albeit at a lesser rate than in the previous years. A sound technological base is being established which will assure the economic viability of a future peaceful Eritrea.

6.2 An Economic Policy for Liberation

Self-reliance is one of the watch-words of the Eritrean revolution. During our visit we were witnesses to the fact that this is no empty slogan but is integral to all the economic activity of the EPLF. At the present time, self-reliance is the means for satisfying the EPLF's material needs. For the future, it is seen as the strategy for improving the overall productive capacity of the Eritrean people and as providing the basis for a non-aligned Eritrea with a high degree of autonomy from external forces.

No country can be independent of external trade relations. There will always be materials that cannot be found locally, and products and machines that cannot be produced economically on the domestic market. The EPLF envisage that an independent Eritrea would promote trade relations based on mutual advantage and seek

economic assistance free of political strings. But it sees trade
restrictions as necessary to maximise the use of local natural resources
and existing skills in order to meet the needs of Eritrean workers
and peasants rather than those of foreign or local owners of large-
scale capital or of feudal landowners (see Appendix 2a EPLF's
National Democratic Programme, Section 2). The EPLF explains
its emphasis on self-reliance in these terms:

> 'In an economically backward Third World country like Eritrea,
> given the domination of world markets by the imperialist countries, this
> policy (of self-reliance) is a necessary precondition for the establishment
> of an independent and developed economy...
>
> The pursuance of a policy of self-reliance is essential for the total
> independence and liberation of a society. Politically it is the only means
> to complete freedom. Economically it is likewise the only means,
> given... prevailing international conditions, that enables a people to
> develop their economic potential depending on their own material and
> human resources. Socially, it is an essential liberating process,
> emphasising as it does working cooperatively and collectively to satisfy
> your own needs. Dependence breeds subservience and lack of self-
> confidence. Freedom from dependence enhances a people's
> independence of thinking, innovativeness, perseverance and pride in
> work and struggle.' (EPLF, Self-Reliance in the Economic Field, 1982).

On our visit we were able to witness the effects of this policy —
the extraordinary self-confidence and inventiveness of the work force,
and the atmosphere of enthusiasm and of cooperative working. In
the EPLF base area the workshops and services we visited were
cooperatives, where workers were discussing the day-to-day problems
of production, receiving further education, or training others. Their
commitment to the EPLF's struggle is a major force in the motivation
and cohesion of these cooperatives. EPLF personnel receive no wages
and we saw no money being used by them during our visit. The EPLF
provides only for its workers' and fighters' basic needs for food,
shelter and health care. Everyone suffers the hardships entailed in
Eritrea's protracted struggle.

The EPLF administers larger areas of liberated territory than
earlier liberation movements in Africa and Latin America. In these
areas it is not only producing for the war effort, but attempting a
far-reaching social transformation. In its own words:

> 'Not only has so much work been done relying on our fighters and
> organised masses, but a rich experience and confidence in organised
> collective work, a new awareness and confidence in being able to
> accomplish feats of amazing and ingenious work relying on one's own
> determined and organised effort, and an understanding of the fact that
> the best and quickest results could be achieved through voluntary
> collective work, has also been gained. The long-term effect of this new
> awareness and confidence is most important, for it will be essential in

the struggle to come to reconstruct and develop our economy, to lay the base for a developed socialist society.' (EPLF, Self-Reliance in the Economic Field, 1982)

6.3 Equipment and Finance

Self-reliance is not only an ideological driving force but also to a large extent an economic necessity. Given the EPLF's current lack of external assistance, it is imperative to minimise any inputs that must be paid for with scarce foreign exchange. The workshops and production units we visited in the base area were remarkable examples of the EPLF's policy in practice, for it was clear that the establishment and running of these workshops involved very little financial cost. The major external costs to the EPLF are: the purchase of fuel to run its extensive transport operation, generators, industrial machines and the mechanised units of the EPLA, the purchase of some heavy ammunition when insufficient supplies are captured, as well as the purchase of food for EPLF personnel.

In spite of some external assistance from sympathetic governments the EPLF says that its main and most regular source of income is from the mass organisations in and outside Eritrea. Inside the country, given the drought and the low level of agricultural production, the main financial source is the clandestine organisation of workers in the occupied Eritrean towns. Outside Eritrea, major funds are provided by the mass organisations in the Middle East, where wages are relatively high. The EPLF mass organisations in Italy, West Germany, Britain and the United States are further important contributors. After our return from Eritrea we witnessed a small example of such fund-raising at a May Day festival organised by the Eritrean Workers' Association in the UK. The EPLF thus operates an extensive voluntary taxation system among the Eritrean diaspora. Since 1980, EPLF taxation on the import and export of goods leaving and entering liberated areas of Eritrea has provided some additional income, as has the commercial use of parts of its lorry fleet in the Sudan whenever there are trucks not being used for the transport of goods into Eritrea.

From Shells to Ploughshares

The vast majority of the materials used by the EPLF is captured from the Ethiopian army in battle, from overrun Ethiopian camps and positions, and from planned raids on Ethiopian-held towns. Ironically, therefore, it is Ethiopia and its foreign backers who are indirectly providing the material support of the Eritrean revolution. The input here is enormous. Apart from some heavy ammunition it is the only source of arms for the EPLF which now fields an army better equipped than most African states. Likewise, the EPLF is serviced by captured trucks, generators, metal and woodworking machines, mobile garages, X-ray units, and sewing machines.

The most remarkable aspect of this captured material is the EPLF's efficiency in using it. Every visitor to the base areas comments on the ingenuity of the workers in the EPLF workshops. Not only are spare parts, cooking utensils, teaching materials, aids for the disabled, and hospital equipment put together from the captured debris of war, but the EPLF is also constructing many of the machines necessary for producing these items. From our own observations the most useful materials are the wood from ammunition boxes, shell and bomb casings, springs and sheet metal from destroyed vehicles. The process is almost literally from shells to ploughshares.

Every available material is put to good use or recycled. The containers in which goods arrive from Port Sudan are used to construct the rooms of the camouflaged buildings in which it is necessary to maintain the dust-free conditions needed for carrying out operations or for housing sensitive equipment. The watches of EPLF fighters are sent back for repair in workshops in the base area. Once totally beyond repair they are stripped and the parts sorted to be used in other watches. Even the black plastic sandals which all EPLF fighters wear are locally produced and then recycled.

Clearly the fact that so much material is captured provides a limitation to the description of the Eritrean economy in the EPLF-held areas as self-reliant. The economy will have to adapt when, with eventual peace, this means of supply is no longer available. Furthermore, with the return of the Eritrean diaspora, this important source of external assistance will no longer be available. However, at that time Eritrea will be in a strong position to attract grants and loans for the reconstruction process from sympathetic governments, and human and material resources currently committed to the war will be free to be reallocated to productive activities.

6.4 Transport and Production

In the early 1970s the EPLF's sole means of transport was camels and donkeys. Building roads in the areas under EPLF control is imperative for the transport of arms and fighters, and with the drought, for the delivery of urgently needed food relief to the local population. By 1975 the EPLF had constructed the 'Liberation Road' — its variant of the Ho Chi Minh trail — stretching from the border with Sudan in the north, through Sahel province and the highlands, to the border with the Ethiopian province of Tigray to the south. A ten-ton load can now be transported from the base area to the trenches of the Halhal or Nacfa front lines overnight. Previously, shifting the same load could take eight days and use 30 camels. The EPLF estimates that the Transport Department has constructed over

'Challenge Road', built by the EPLF in 1982, has 37 hairpin bends in 12 kms.

1,000 kilometres of road through rugged mountainous terrain.

With the limited technology at the EPLF's disposal, some of these roads represent major feats of engineering. The most dramatic route we travelled was the 'Challenge Road', cut in 1982 into the precipitous eastern slopes of the Sahel mountains to give direct access to the North East Sahel front. This road twists and winds its way from valley floor to mountain ridge with 37 hairpins built over fortress-like supporting walls in a stretch 12 kilometers long. Swiss engineers, in peacetime, without air attack, would be proud of it.

With our particular interest in economic development in the EPLF areas, we made a point of visiting the workshops and production units which we describe in this section. All were hidden under thick thorn trees to avoid air attacks from Ethiopian planes. The camouflage was often so effective that, save for the muted sound of whirring engines and machines or the banging of hammers against metal, we could have been walking in a deserted valley. The experience of leaving nomads in a hot and arid valley to enter a large area cut into the hillside full of shining machines and a skilled work force was not merely dramatic. It was moving at a step from medieval to modern times. The skill levels are illustrated by the She'eb vehicle repair garage — a number of different but related workshops. The garage is one of a network which services, repairs and rebuilds the EPLF's transport fleet. In She'eb only civilian vehicles are

Women operating a lathe in the workshops of the EPLF base area.

overhauled. It has 150 full-time trained staff, half of whom work with mobile repair units in more remote areas. Those responsible for individual workshops have university qualifications in mechanical engineering, and 65% of the workforce has over ten years garage experience mainly from past jobs in the Eritrean towns or abroad. A high proportion, particularly among the younger workers, are women — we estimated one in four overall. For example, at the workshops. five girls aged between 12 and 14 were training in the electrical repair shop. The She'eb workshops also serve as the main training area for mechanics, who follow two-year courses. We met a number of students from the Revolution School (see Chapter 9), who were being given basic engineering experience.

The technology in the workshops was sophisticated and included a number of lathes, drills, saws, a truck brake tester and electrical testing equipment. One of the engineers at She'eb estimated that they could make 60% of the vehicle spare parts in their own workshops. The majority of the machines which the workshops used had been made by themselves. This included a power saw, a metal planing machine, a hydraulic press, metal grinders, an angular metal-bending machine, a tubular metal-bending machine and a forge. They were constructed from a variety of materials including broken truck springs, chassis members, tank armour, shell casings and the lead from truck batteries. The ingenuity of the mechanics was plain to see — Land Rovers, criticised for being under-powered, were being

The EPLF make many of their own machines. This rectifier makes use of welded shell casings.

fitted with more powerful 6-cylinder Toyota engines, while their own engines were bored out to increase their cylinder capacity from 1600 cc. to 2400 cc. and fitted with larger diameter Toyota pistons.

Suakin Garage is situated in Sudan, south of the main port of Port Sudan. This garage maintains the transport fleet that brings supplies, particularly emergency food, from the port to Eritrea. The garage is extensive, employing 55 full-time mechanics, 15 of whom are women. Even after our arrival after dusk it was a hive of activity. At any one time around 15 trucks are being given a complete overhaul taking four days, while a further 10 are undergoing a day-long service to ensure a trouble-free return to Eritrea. In spite of difficulties in obtaining spare parts, trucks are extremely well maintained to squeeze the maximum use from them. The workshop was well equipped. Many of the machines had been captured during the course of the war, including the two large generators, removed from the Eritrean towns of Decamhare and Keren, which power the whole complex.

'Vodka-Cola' Trucks

At Suakin the inventiveness of the Eritrean revolution was again transparent. Normal trucks were being converted into oil tankers on site with the containers built from sheets of scrap metal. Trucks were being re-assembled using parts originating from different countries, with 'engine swapping' commonplace. The workers describe the hybrid results as 'Vodka-Cola' trucks since most of the vehicles supplied to the Ethiopian government were American up to 1974 and Soviet after 1977. One of the workshop's home-made creations was a tyre vulcanising machine for retreading truck tyres. The Suakin mechanics had simply copied the principle from an imported model and built one themselves, which now operates adjacent to the original machine.

We also visited a number of other workshops and production units in the base area. The watches of EPLF fighters are fixed in an underground watch repair shop. This service, like all others, is free. Broken watches are collected from the EPLF units, including those operating behind the Ethiopian lines. They are registered and marked, so that they can eventually be returned to the same individual, and sent to this workshop which is run by 28 staff, most of whom have been disabled in the fighting. A few staff had watch-repairing skills before they joined the EPLF and are now teaching their skills to others. We interviewed one woman who had lost her leg in battle in 1980. After two years' rehabilitation in the camp for the disabled at Orota, she began work in this workshop. She told us that the work provided an essential outlet for her energies and for her determination to continue to contribute to the revolution in spite of her serious injuries. She also spends three hours a day

Workshops, clinics and schools are heavily camouflaged against air attack. This is the EPLF's watch repair workshop.

studying for higher school grades.

The radio repair workshop consists of a complex of three separate workshops — one maintains the EPLF's wireless communication equipment, another fixes personal radios and cassette recorders, and the third carries out research and training. The workers we met were remarkably well informed about world affairs and told us the BBC World Service provides their main source of information. They were well aware of the sympathetic stance of the British Labour Party regarding the EPLF and told us that fighters in the trenches had stayed up to follow both the 1979 and 1983 British General Election results as they emerged. They also showed an avid interest in other topical changes of political power abroad, such as in the succession of Chernenko in the USSR and in the US presidential elections.

The radio workshops were staffed by highly qualified technicians — six of those we met had university degrees. The radio repair training centre has so far provided four month courses with a further four month follow-up for 80 trainees who had already been radio operators in the field and had at least tenth grade education. They would subsequently work either at workshops on the front line or become 'barefoot technicians' able to do on-the-spot repairs even during battle.

The printing photographic and cinematographic workshops are all sub-sections of the EPLF Information Department. In the Printing Section we were shown the range of materials published by the EPLF, who estimate that they have produced some 200,000 copies of 72 different textbooks for EPLF schools, adult education classes and technical courses (see Chapter 9). Examples of these textbooks are displayed around the walls of the section from which orders are despatched. Primary education is in the Tigrinya and Tigre languages, but publications are also produced in the languages of the Afar and Kunama nationalities. A magazine is produced in Amharic, the official language of Ethiopia, for the Ethiopian prisoners of war held by the EPLF. Leaflets in Amharic are produced aimed at persuading the Ethiopian troops in Eritrea of the justice of the EPLF's struggle. These leaflets also are left in places where the Ethiopian army is likely to find them.

The Photographic Section is well equipped with basic darkroom equipment. Teams of Information Department journalists and photographers follow developments all over Eritrea. Their photographs are printed and used in the EPLF's magazines and publications, and photographic exhibitions are sent to the front lines and to the EPLF offices abroad. We were shown photos of the recent EPLF victories at Tessenei and Mersa Teklai, and at the time of our visit the Cinematographic Section was busy editing a video film of the battle of Mersa Teklai. Copies of the video film of the capture

The Information Department edits the video of the EPLF's victory on the NE Sahel front.

of Tessenei have already been sent to the EPLF mass organisations in Europe.

The EPLF have set up a number of plants for processing food. These include flour mills, often powered by engines from damaged Ethiopian trucks, and bakeries for which the base area workshops have designed and built both electric and diesel heated ovens. The latter have reduced cooking time and led to important savings in scarce firewood. Reflecting the Italian past, a spaghetti unit is operating in the camp for the displaced and produces around 50 kilograms a day, covering a portion of local needs and providing some nutritional variety to the diet.

EPLF fighters have no uniform, although most carry at least one item of captured military clothing — a shirt or a pair of trousers, or a belt or some leggings. The one identifying feature of the EPLF fighter is black plastic sandals. A small factory, set up in the base area in 1979 now produces 600 to 650 pairs daily. Black PVC granules are fed into one end of an Italian injection-moulding machine, while the sandals are stamped out at the other. All that remains is to fix the metal buckle.

PVC is expensive and difficult to obtain and transport from the European suppliers. EPLF fighters make temporary repairs with a hot knife blade to make their sandals last longer; but when they are

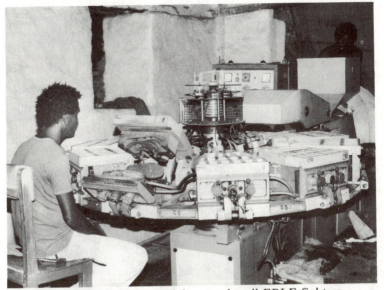

Making the black plastic sandals worn by all EPLF fighters.

finally beyond repair, the sandals are collected from the different EPLF units to be recycled. The base area workshops have designed and made machines which wash these used sandals, chop them into small pieces and granulate them. The raw material used for new sandals is then a 50-50 mix of new granules and recycled granules. Some sandals have been supplied to the displaced people in the camps run by ERA, and plans are under way to extend production to supply other sectors of the Eritrean civilian population.

Sanitary Towel Production

While the sandal factory can be seen as an example of EPLF import substitution, this is not the case for the EPLF's factory for producing sanitary towels, a product which previously had been used only by a tiny elite of educated urban women. The bulk of the population had to make do with much less hygienic methods. Tigre women in the lowlands, following traditional taboos, sit inside a tent sited over absorbent sand when menstruating. They would prepare food for the family in this tent and pass the prepared meal under the flap of the tent to the men outside.

In such a context the mass production and distribution of sanitary towels is revolutionary. This apparently simple measure is transforming both the self-image and the role of Eritrean women.

Sanitary towel machine bought with funds from the National Women's Associations of Europe.

The machine for producing sanitary towels was bought with funds raised by the National Unions of Eritrean Women in Europe, who continue to provide the funds to buy raw materials. Production started in February 1984 and the modern machine now produces at a rate of around 9,000 towels per hour. Before machine production was introduced, sanitary towels were hand made with gauze and Sudanese raw cotton by teams of women from the camps for the displaced. EPLF women fighters are the first to be supplied, but sanitary towels are slowly being introduced to the local (nomadic) population of the base area. When stocks have been built up the EPLF will produce for the civilian population in other areas. The Hygiene Department which is responsible for this factory also has plans to develop local soap production. The Department has qualified chemists with the necessary experience but has yet to find a source for raw materials.

In spite of the severe difficulties imposed by the war, the EPLF has established a substantial light industrial sector in the base areas. Industrial development in Eritrea will face a very different set of problems when a peaceful solution is finally found. But the EPLF's achievements to date provide a strong argument within the overall case for the economic viability of a future self-governing Eritrea.

CHAPTER 7

Food and Famine

Agriculture is central to Eritrea's economy. Four fifths of the population earn their living from the land, either from settled agriculture or from livestock rearing. Now, following years of intermittent drought and war, food production in Eritrea is in crisis, and reports are reaching the outside world of population displacement and famine. Our own visit, needing to assess the severity of this situation, looked at how the EPLF is coping with the emergency. But the famine must also be put in the overall context of food production in Eritrea.

7.1 Agriculture in Crisis

Farming in Eritrea faces three major problems. The first is that the feudal relations up to the 1970s impoverished the landless and poor peasants, and caught them in a cycle of hunger, disease and debt. Second, throughout the colonial period Eritrean production had been insufficient to feed the whole population. Imports, whether from Ethiopia or from Sudan, have been necessary for many years. Third, Eritrea lies in the Sahelian rainfall zone of Africa and Eritrean agriculture is vulnerable to frequent years of drought. The current famine, caused in part by the drought conditions of the last four years, is discussed later in this section.

Eritrea has three major agricultural regions, of which the largest is the lowlands to the east and west of the central highland area (see Map 3). With an elevation of up to 600 metres, the lowlands are flat or undulating with fertile soil but little rainfall. With the exception of a few irrigation schemes, mainly in the east, most of the crops are rain-fed. Sorghum, sesame, cotton, maize and beans are grown. Some regions produce surpluses which in the past provided the towns with grain.

The second area, the Green Belt, is a narrow strip running between the eastern lowlands and the highlands, which receives rain twice a year enabling a wider variety of crops to be grown. Agriculture here is more intensive and maize, coffee and some vegetables are cultivated.

Finally, the highlands above 1500 metres have a cooler climate and sufficient rain to allow, in normal years, the cultivation of wheat, barley, millet, teff (a grain specific to this part of Africa) and maize.

All available land is used and family plots are relatively small — most being between one and four hectares. Erosion has been a major problem. Over-utilisation and grazing of the soil cover has left the earth exposed. On the steep slopes the topsoil is washed away by the infrequent, but short and heavy rains.

The Italians developed estates and commercial farms in parts of the lowlands and some agricultural mechanisation was introduced. But elsewhere in Eritrea farming has remained at the level of peasant subsistence production using rudimentary techniques. Wooden ploughs with either wooden or iron blades are drawn by oxen or camels. Sowing, weeding and harvesting is done by hand using the simplest of tools.

Although her mineral wealth may prove more important in the distant future, agriculture is still Eritrea's main economic resource, and developing self-sufficiency is an EPLF priority. How realistic is this, given a predominantly peasant production and Eritrea's recent history of cereal deficits? There are four ways in which Eritrea's food production can be boosted: (1) through land redistribution; (2) through technical improvements; (3) through expanding the areas under cultivation; and (4) through prioritising food for the basic needs of local consumption over other agricultural production. Some of these measures are already being implemented in the areas under EPLF control.

Land Redistribution

A description of the first phase of the EPLF's land reform was given in Chapter 2. The second phase envisages the reorganisation of production, and anticipates 'cooperatives' in which farmers pool their existing individual plots to farm the land together. So far, most cooperatives have been established on land allocated by the local land distribution committee. The more usual form of cooperation is through 'mutual assistance teams', where poor peasants who have received land on adjacent plots during the land reform, share tools, oxen and labour. In the recent years of drought, mutual aid teams have become an important structure for the distribution of seeds and tools in programmes launched by the Eritrean Relief Association to prevent destitute peasants leaving the land.

It still remains to be seen how cooperatives and organised large-scale production will develop under the EPLF. Certainly the experience of the Ethiopian government's state farms has not been positive, but these have often involved forced recruitment of workers, highly authoritarian management, and low wages. Some of the former foreign-run commercial farms in Eritrea, particularly in the Gash-Setit area, are being run with some success by the EPLF and are providing some of the food needed by the front. However, the conversion of small-scale peasant production into larger farms may well not be welcomed by peasants whose social security in times of drought has been their ownership of land. In the future, the provision of food and credit to cooperatives during periods of drought may help overcome poor peasants' attachment to individual plots. In addition, the eventual return of refugees from Sudan could provide a workforce, already separated from traditional land holdings, for future large farms on newly exploited land.

Technical Progress

Food production in Eritrea is being increased through technical improvements both in farming and on the land itself. The link with redistribution is crucial to the EPLF's success. Otherwise, as the experience of other countries suggests, such as that of India during the 'Green Revolution', technical improvements help wealthier farmers and landowners at the expense of poorer farmers, who lack the resources to pay for the agricultural inputs or are unable to repay their loans.

In 1975 the EPLF set up its Agriculture Department with numerous qualified agronomists, foresters and veterinary doctors. This has been able to make a significant impact in spite of the lack of resources. An EPLF agricultural and technical school has been established. Each village committee selects a local person to attend the basic course which covers agronomy, animal husbandry and the

Agricultural class, Marib, Serae Province.

production and repair of simple agricultural implements. At the time of our visit we were told that nearly 700 peasants had received this education and were acting as extension agents in their local communities.

The Agricultural Department has been active in making available local tools through providing the necessary equipment and training for the formation of local blacksmith cooperatives. Some twenty of these cooperatives now exist making ploughs, hoes and scythes which are sold at prices well below those of the local market. Such tools have also been distributed free to mutual assistance teams of the poorest farmers, whom the Agriculture Department also provide with chemicals for treating seed and storage of grains, as well as the training to ensure their safe use. Once better rains return such measures are likely to cut grain losses significantly. In future, the Agricultural Department hopes to exploit Eritrea's mineral wealth in potash as a fertiliser, and to make available improved seed varieties adapted to the local conditions of soil and rainfall.

In the displaced people's camps, poultry production cooperatives have already been established. We saw a unit in the Solomuna camp for which the EPLF workshops, in characteristically inventive fashion, have made an incubator which is plumbed to a boiler and has the capacity to hatch 3,000 fertilised eggs at a time.

The Veterinary Section of the Agriculture Department also has been active in training and equipping teams of 'barefoot vets'. Five such teams are now operating , providing vaccination and basic curative services to both the nomadic population and the settled population, for whom oxen are vital for ploughing. But these teams face a mammoth task during the current drought as animals, weakened by hunger, are being decimated by epidemics of rinderpest and anthrax.

A Forestry, Soil and Water Section has been established to protect the environment against erosion and reduction in soil fertility. Work is beginning on terracing, afforestation and the management of surface water through building small dams in the gullies. This latter work, which we saw in progress, is vital for the long-term agricultural security of Eritrea. It is especially relevant for the highland areas where erosion and soil exhaustion is already far advanced. But it is difficult to undertake the large-scale works needed while the fighting continues, since such schemes immediately become targets for air attack. This underlines how important it is for Eritrea's future livelihood that a peaceful solution is found before the ecological destruction becomes irreversible.

New Land

To boost its food production Eritrea can expand the area under

Mike Goldwater /NETWORK

Villagers in Adi-Sesa, southern Eritrea, construct dam walls to hold back water for irrigation when the rains come.

cultivation. The eastern lowlands provide the most potential, as the highlands are already overcrowded and over-farmed. In the east, six rivers flood onto the coastal plain, allowing large areas at the bottom of the escarpment to be cultivated. In a year of reasonable rainfall, this area is very productive and can produce four crops a year. Production here was traditionally organised through agricultural committees which allocated the tasks of maintaining the earth barriers and directing the water flow to the different plots. This structure provides a good base for future collective organisation and important technical improvements can be made by replacing the earth dams with 'gabions' — wire mesh boxes filled with stones. In the western lowlands, agricultural potential is considerable in the areas around Tessenei and Om Hager.

A recent estimate gives a potential cultivable area in Eritrea of at least six and a half million acres. Three million acres were under cultivation by 1970. This is four times more than the figure provided by the British to the UN in 1950, on the basis of which Eritrea was characterised as economically unviable. A recent commentator has proposed that, were Eritrea's agricultural potential fully exploited, it would be able 'to provide not only for its own requirements but to serve as a potential breadbasket for the neighbouring Arab and African markets.' (Araia Tseggai 1983). Not least, this unused potential could be put to use to provide work and food for the bulk of the returning refugee population. A further important food potential for Eritrea is coastal fishing in the Red Sea. But with the war it has gone severely into decline.

Basic Needs

Eritrea's ability to meet the basic food needs of its population depends on the prioritising of food crops for local consumption, as against non-food crops for local use and cash crops for export. The plantations established in the Italian period mainly produced cash crops for the Italian market. In order to avoid imports, Britain sought to make Eritrea self-sufficient in grain, fruit and vegetables. Under this policy the grain harvest quadrupled between 1939 and 1946. (Trevaskis 1960).

After Eritrea's annexation in 1962, the Ethiopian regime made increasing use of the region as a source of foreign exchange, and concentrated on the cultivation of fruit and vegetables for export while local grain production declined markedly. Those plantations which are now farmed by the EPLF continue to produce fruit and vegetables, but for the needs of the front and the local population. In the future, the EPLF plan to prioritise the plantation areas for local food and for the production of raw materials necessary for development of local industry. The example we were given was that locally produced cotton could supply an EPLF textile factory for which there are already skilled Eritrean workers, as much of the labour force of the Barattolo cotton factory is now in EPLF-held areas.

In conclusion, Eritrea has immense potential to develop its own food production, although much of its current production is threatened by over-cultivation. To put food production in Eritrea back on its feet after the years of war and drought, large-scale programmes are needed — to arrest the erosion and to utilise the unused potential. Such projects will require major grants and loans, and many can only start when they are secure from military attack or sabotage. Peace is a precondition for an Eritrea free from famine.

7.2 The Current Famine

In common with other countries in the Sahelian climatic zone, Eritrea has a long experience of periods of drought and poor harvests. To some extent Eritrea's agricultural economy has adapted to this. There is a yearly migration to Sudan of poorer farmers who supplement their income by wage labour in the 'Green Triangle' of the fertile grain-producing area to the south of Khartoum.

The Eritrean peasant farmer can usually cope with the problems caused by a single isolated harvest failure, as in a good year surpluses are stored as a safeguard against bad years, and there may be some cash savings from past work of a family member as a migrant labourer. The difficulties become severe if there is drought for any longer. If drought persists, a vicious circle sets in. Family food stocks run down, self-rationing is imposed and people eat less. The heavy work of cultivation becomes increasingly onerous, and farmers weakened by malnourishment may have to cut back on the areas cultivated. When little is left of the family's grain, and when cash savings are depleted, farmers may have little alternative but to consume the grain put aside as seed and sell oxen and tools, leading to a reduced harvest the following year. After the 1974 famine in northern Ethiopia, only half of the land usually cultivated was sown in 1975.

In the early 1920s four successive years of drought led to a massive famine and the death of up to a third of Eritrea's population. Now, 60 years later, Eritrea is once again in the grip of a major famine. The activities of the relevant EPLF Departments and of the Eritrean Relief Association (ERA), who are responsible for the relief operation in the EPLF-administered areas, have had to be prioritised towards 'emergency' programmes.

Poor Rains

Rainfall in Eritrea has been poor for 8 of the 14 years since 1970. In particular, large tracts of Eritrea faced drought in 1980, 1981, 1982 and 1983. While some villagers harvested practically nothing in all four years, most would have harvested some grain in one or two of these years, but not nearly enough to cover a family's basic needs. 1983 appears to have been a particularly bad year for Eritrea's peasant farmers. An aid worker who visited a normally surplus-producing area in western Eritrea in October 1983 reported:

'Quite striking is the fact that all along the route from Kassala (in Sudan, near the border with Eritrea) to Shelalo there is evidence of inadequate rainfall and subsequent poor harvests. Huge plots of cultivatable land planted in May or June show no crop growth at all, and in many cases one can see tiny seedlings of less than 3 inches that have withered and died.' (Smith 1983).

Two months later an ERA report summed up the situation:

'In the last rainy season, in the areas covered by the first rainy season, the rains were extremely poor and did not come at the right time. In the beginning of June, it started to rain in many parts of these areas. However from mid-June up to the end of July, very crucial periods for

Mike Goldwater/NETWORK

These wild pods are all this family has to eat. They must be boiled for hours to destroy the poisons present.

cultivation, there was virtually no rain in most parts of the areas covered by the first rainy season. Furthermore, the rains that came after July were inadequate and did not last long enough for late crops. Consequently a large part of the country was left barren with little or no harvest... The condition of the people is bad and is growing more serious by the day. People have little or nothing to eat. In many of the drought-stricken areas it is not uncommon to see people trying to subsist on roots and wild fruit, some of which are not fit for human consumption.' (ERA 1983).

Independent observers from European voluntary agencies later substantiated that many starving Eritreans were reduced to eating berries. Even Eritreans with some savings were becoming increasingly hard pressed. Both the traditional surplus producing areas of south western Eritrea and the grain-growing areas of Sudan had experienced harvest failures in 1983. At the time of our visit, grain in Eritrea had more than doubled in price to 125 birr (£45) for a 100 kg sack, with which a family of five could survive for only six weeks. Official statistics estimate per capita income in Ethiopia and Eritrea at £100 per year. In Gedaref in Sudan, prices had reached a highest ever figure of 41 Sudanese pounds (£23) per sack, so that those Eritreans who had successfully found work on Sudanese farms could send back much less grain for their efforts.

Effects of the War

But in many areas the war is having a more serious effect on food production than the drought. During our trip we were informed of many ways in which the military conflict was creating difficulties for farmers and grazers alike. Farmers near the Ethiopian-held areas risk losing their crop and food stocks during advances by Ethiopian forces, and time and labour must be spent to make safe hiding places for food and other possessions (see also Eisenloefell & Ronnback 1983). The seventh Ethiopian offensive of 1983, in which the Ethiopian army, over a six month period, made thrusts into Barka and Senhit provinces, severely disrupted the farming and led farmers to abandon cultivation and flee to safer areas.

In April 1983, the Ethiopian government announced compulsory military service. Many young peasants were forcibly drafted into the army, while others fled to Sudan. By early 1984 the Khartoum office of the United Nations High Commissioner for Refugees reported that 300 people a day were fleeing to Sudan from Eritrea and Ethiopia to join the 300,000 Eritrean and 150,000 Ethiopian refugees already living there. Many of these refugees were young people avoiding conscription. Conscription also had the effect of limiting the sale of grain between better-off and worse-off areas, as peasants were afraid to come to Ethiopian controlled market towns.

Ethiopian air bombardment, too, is causing many problems. Livestock herds are targets of bombing raids over EPLF-held territory, and we were told that over the years many thousands of cattle, camels, goats and sheep have been killed in such attacks. Agricultural work is constrained by the risk of air attack, particularly near the front lines, where work in the fields must be done at night. The effect is to reduce the area that can be cultivated and the quality of the cultivation.

The war limits the movement of the nomads' herds, thereby adding to the problems in specific areas of over-grazing and water scarcity. Large tracts of grass or crops are burnt to deny the guerrillas place for concealment. The mines left by Ethiopian troops when they abandon military positions are a danger both to grazing livestock and to the herders themselves. The EPLF try to clear these mines, but this is a time-consuming and labour-intensive process. The ERA told us that the villagers of two districts of Serae province abandoned attempts to farm their land because their fields had been mined by the Ethiopian army.

In the coastal areas, trading and fishing is heavily restricted by the Ethiopians, who police with naval patrol boats. The ERA have recorded that 9,500 people have left three fishing villages in the Danakil (mainly to Sudan and Saudi Arabia) because of the restrictions on their only means of livelihood (ERA 1983).

A Million in Need

The ERA also has produced detailed information on the extent and severity of the famine according to the numbers in each village in need of food assistance. Their overall picture indicated that well over a million people in the areas administered by the EPLF would need food assistance in 1984. This figure does not include those in the areas of Ethiopian administration. About a third of the ERA figure is in the provinces which are almost entirely under EPLF control — with over a third of a million in the Sahel and Barka provinces. The remainder are in the contested areas, with the highest concentrations in the highland provinces, where population densities are also greatest.

The figures warn of an incipient famine of dramatic proportions unless urgent action is taken. Behind the statistics for 'those in need of food assistance' are individuals — particularly women and children — wasting from malnourishment and accompanying ill health. ERA reports the incidence of malaria, tuberculosis and dysentery to be rapidly on the increase. Death from starvation has become increasingly common.

The ERA figures also indicate the extent to which the nomadic population has suffered from the drought. Weakened by insufficient

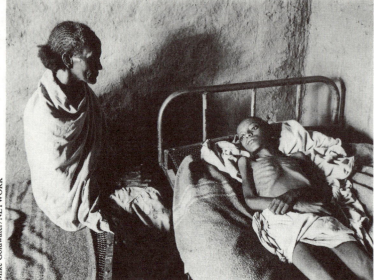

Mike Goldwater/NETWORK

The drought affected an estimated 1.2 million Eritreans in 1984.
This ten year old boy is suffering from severe malnutrition in
Maiduba clinic, Serae province.

grazing and lack of water, their animals have become increasingly
prone to disease. Thousands of animals have already died and many
herders have lost nine-tenths of their livestock. In Adobeha, a district
of Sahel province through which we passed, a recent ERA study
showed that average animal ownership has decreased from a pre-1980
level of 34 goats, 4 sheep, 2.4 cattle, 1.0 camels and 0.48 donkeys
per person to a level of 6.5 goats, 0.46 sheep, 0.18 cattle, 0.14 camels
and 0.08 donkeys per person in 1983. This represents overall losses
of between 80 and 90% of the livestock in this area. For the settled
farming population, oxen are essential for ploughing and represent
a peasant family's most prized possession. The death or sickness of
an animal severely undermines the ability of poorer farmers to
cultivate the land. Animals must be rented and the owner must be
repaid at harvest time in grain. If the harvest is bad, poor farmers
are quickly driven into debt.

Lack of drinking water is becoming critical over much of Eritrea.
The wells we saw in Sahel province were either completely dry or
were supplying only a fraction of the water of previous years. With
two months to go before the main rains were expected, water was
already strictly rationed; áfter the quantities needed for drinking and
cooking, little was left for washing and personal hygiene. The nursery
for orphans at Solomuna camp was suffering severe problems. The

Well digging in Sahel province. This is an urgent priority in areas where wells are drying up, forcing the population to leave.

possibility of moving the children to another site with a better supply of water was being investigated. The Revolution School nearby had not reopened a month after the half-term break because of the water shortages.

A senior water resources engineer sent by War on Want to Eritrea in March 1984 wrote in his report:

'The 1983 drought was particularly severe and it was estimated that close to 200,000 people in Sahel and Barka regions of Eritrea were affected. Present indications (March 1984) suggest that the 1984 drought is already potentially more severe than that of 1983. Water rationing has already started in many areas (two to three months earlier than in 1983) and unless substantial rains arrive by May the water situation will become very serious. If the rains arrive late in July as they did in 1983 the situation will be extremely serious in most areas.' (E. Thomas, Halcrow Water, 1984).

Lack of drinking water is the main reason for people leaving their villages. Given that a peasant family's only source of livelihood is the land, this decision is only taken when there really is no other choice. In the highlands so many wells have dried up that fetching water now often involves walking three to four hours. In one village it was reported that water was rationed so that a family of five would receive 20 litres to last five days, or about 1.5 pints per person per day. ERA are running 12 camps for displaced people whose total population now exceeds 70,000. This figure includes people who have fled from the war zones as well as from villages suffering from water and food scarcity. But the people in these camps at the moment make up only a small proportion of the vast numbers — estimated by ERA at over half a million — who have been displaced within Eritrea since the fighting began.

We interviewed women who had left their villages in Serae province when the water supply became insufficient for even the most minimal needs of the village population. A typical story is that of Abrahet whom we spoke to in Solomuna camp in northern Sahel province.

The Story of Abrahet

For the last four years in Abrahet's village of Adi Gutkhula (in Guhtchea district of Serae province) the harvest has been very poor. In 1980 and 1981 Abrahet's family harvested small quantities, but in 1982 they harvested nothing. In 1983 the rains started in August but proved insufficient and again nothing was harvested. Over these years most villagers completely depleted all their reserves of grain. Those who had relatives in Asmara received some outside help in money or grain. Others just had to beg from those who had food. ERA had only been able to distribute small quantities. One such distribution, made in August 1983, gave a family of seven a hundred kilo sack of grain. But this would scarcely last a month. No Ethiopian government distribution had ever taken place in the village. By September 1983 Abrahet's family had sold their ploughing oxen and other possessions. Water problems were becoming more and more severe. The children in the village were suffering badly from malnutrition. Unable to resist disease, many were dying.

In October, Abrahet left her village on foot with her two children along with 27 other families, carrying only the clothes they were wearing as everything else had been sold. She walked for two days to Maidema; from there she found a truck to Adi Tseta and another to the Mareb area where ERA run temporary transit camps and provide food. She stayed in this area for some 6 months before moving again to Solomuna camp where we met her. She told us she had heard that, of the original population of 400 families in her village, only 20 had stayed on. Those who had left had gone to find work wherever they heard reports that there had been some rain. Many left Eritrea altogether to go to Sudan or to the western part of Tigray province in Ethiopia, where harvests have been relatively good for the last few years. According to ERA's statistics 8,250 people abandoned their villages in Guhtchea district in 1983.

In summary, Eritrea's population is heading for a major crisis — around a third of the population face increasing malnutrition and disease and need food assistance. Already large numbers have fled their homes and many have died. Outside assistance is urgently needed.

7.3 The Scandal in Relief Assistance

There is no disagreement about the severity of the food and water shortages in Eritrea. The figures released by the Ethiopian government through its Relief and Rehabilitation Commission (RRC) broadly substantiate ERA's own description of the scale of the problems. The RRC estimated grain yields for the 1983 harvest in the vicinity of the Eritrean capital, Asmara, to be less than one-sixth of average yields. In the RRC's report for 1984 they estimate 827,000 people in need of assistance in Eritrea. But the RRC does not publicly admit that they have no access to most of Eritrea.

As reports on the scale of the famine become wider known, more relief agencies accept that relief must go through channels other than the RRC and the voluntary agencies operating in the Ethiopian-held areas. Few, however, have spelt out these facts to the public. The International Committee of the Red Cross (ICRC) made front page news of the difficulties of bringing relief assistance to the affected areas. Carrying the headline 'Ethiopia — Over a Million Disaster Victims Out of Reach', the ICRC bulletin of May 1984 reported:

'Insecurity in many areas and the logistical problem of moving large amounts of food around a mountainous and underdeveloped country have left large sections of the civilian population especially in Eritrea, Tigray and north Wollo without hope of aid and on the brink of starvation. Relief workers operating in Eritrea and Tigray say children are already dying in large numbers.'

No mention is made by the Red Cross of the existence of ERA and its ability to reach those 'out of reach' in Eritrea. The Ethiopian government can enforce this silence on those agencies who have personnel in Ethiopia because the agencies fear action being taken against their programmes if they make the full facts known.

Our own conclusions on the question of access to famine victims are based on conversations with independent agency officials both before and after our visit, and with ERA officials in Eritrea, on interviews with Eritreans displaced by the drought and on the reports of both the RRC and agencies working inside Ethiopia. Firstly, we believe EPLF claims of administering 85% of the area of Eritrea to be likely to be accurate. These are the rural areas where the population most directly affected by the drought lives. For a number of reasons only a small number of these people will reach the RRC distribution points, which are limited to the Ethiopian-controlled towns. The route may be blocked by the military front lines, and the distances involved may be very large. The poorest farmers have neither the animals needed to carry the grain nor the money to rent them. Farmers are very reluctant to go to the towns, which are garrisons for the Ethiopian army, for fear of forced conscription. Peasants from the EPLF areas risk being turned back as they cannot produce the documentation to prove that they are members of an Ethiopian-sponsored peasant association.

ERA's Distribution Efficiency...

In spite of the difficulties ERA face, their relief programme is efficient and well-organised. Sorghum is bought in the eastern province of Sudan while food and medicines from the West are delivered by ship to Port Sudan. We saw the extensive base near Suakin which acts as a transit depot. Convoys of lorries transport the supplies to stores and distribution points in Eritrea. We saw such a convoy entering Eritrea, each lorry laden with 10 tons of grain. A dozen passengers were perched high on top of the sacks, as the lorries double up as the EPLF's public transport system.

The lorries are well-maintained and receive a service after every journey on their return to the garage at Suakin. There is no evidence of the abandoned and broken-down trucks which have so often characterised emergency relief operations elsewhere. On the contrary, the EPLF is able to repair its vehicles and manufacture many spare

ERA trucks bring in sacks of grain from Port Sudan, April 1984.

parts which, if imported, would be slow in arriving or difficult to obtain. The EPLF has developed a comprehensive network of roads which are serviced by 'petrol stations' — a single pump and tank carefully hidden under trees.

From the main distribution points, trucks deliver to the local relief committees. In more remote areas or in the areas beyond the Ethiopian lines where it is risky to take vehicles, food is transported on camels or mules. ERA's policy is to distribute food directly to the villages, so that farmers are encouraged to stay to cultivate next year's crop and thus avoid large-scale displacement which would have disastrous consequences for future food production.

The relief committees, which are part of the elected local People's Assemblies, assess the numbers in need, report their situation to ERA, and take responsibility for local distribution if and when the grain arrives. With poorer farmers well represented on these committees they are able to ensure the most needy are given priority. However, the amount ERA has had to distribute meets only a fraction of real needs. The committees must continually revise their lists by applying more stringent criteria so that only the most desperate receive assistance (Eisenloefell and Ronnback 1983).

...and Funding Crisis

ERA told us that the amount of relief assistance they had received in the first four months of 1984 amounted to only US $2.7 million.

This represents a mere 8% of ERA's emergency relief budget, which itself is calculated on only 30% of the total numbers of those in need. The effect of these serious shortfalls is already to be seen.

Major structural damage to Eritrean agriculture has already occurred, and it is imperative for the future prosperity of the area that this be halted. Food relief will be needed for a number of years to come even with the return of good rains. The extensive well-digging programme, for which the EPLF Construction Department is urgently seeking funds, should be given high priority. Assistance to these 'emergency' programmes must be accompanied by assistance to ERA's longer-term programmes to help the poorer farmers re-acquire tools and oxen, without being driven into the vicious circle of debt.

The quantity of aid ERA currently receives is small because the major donors — governments and the large multilateral agencies — either are not contributing or are only channelling relatively small sums through the voluntary agencies.

A report in 1983 commissioned by a group of British voluntary agencies showed that 30 times more emergency aid was being sent to official Ethiopian channels than was sent to the agencies distributing in the areas controlled by the fronts.

This distorted allocation of emergency humanitarian assistance cries out for a radical response from aid donors — especially governments who do not face the diplomatic constraints of some international agencies. But there also is the Ethiopian government's controversial — if not scandalous — record on food aid distribution. Much evidence has now come to light indicating that the Ethiopian government feeds its army with food aid granted on the basis of famine appeals. What we saw during our own trip added to this evidence. As already indicated, at Mersa Teklai, at the site of the Ethiopian army quarters, and miles from any drought refugees, we found cartons containing tins of butter-oil marked 'Gift of the European Economic Community to the People of Ethiopia'.

The questions raised over the last twelve months by this kind of evidence have yet to be satisfactorily answered in spite of the investigation missions sent to Addis. The Ethiopian RRC say they exchange imported food aid for other local products in government stores, and that these local products are then distributed to the needy population. But satisfactory accounts of this procedure have yet to be produced and unless donors protest strongly at these practices they are open to the justified suspicion of giving military not humanitarian assistance, and in this case of adding to, rather than relieving, the sufferings of the famine victims.

At the time of writing the outlook for the Eritrean population is bleak. Unless governmental assistance massively supplements the efforts of the voluntary agencies in helping ERA there will be a short and long term disaster. Those who die in a famine are always the poorest groups, and a third of the Eritrean population is already threatened. If ERA does not receive immediate supplies and transport assistance on a major scale there is not only the risk of mass starvation but also mass emigration to neighbouring Sudan, already suffering food shortages of its own. Eritrea also needs massive assistance in the longer term to reverse the devastation of its agriculture. It is imperative for the international community to act with aid, rather than simply analyse and sympathise.

CHAPTER 8

A National Health Service

The radical changes that the EPLF is bringing about in health care must be seen in the context of its broader strategy to alter the structures of society in favour of the most oppressed. In the field of health this means a commitment to reach the groups most neglected by the health services of Eritrea's colonial past — the more remote communities, the nomads, and women. With the acute hardships created by the war and the drought, Eritrea is probably suffering worse health than all but a couple of other Third World countries. Less than half the children survive to adulthood and of these half will die before the age of forty.

Against this horrific background the EPLF's Health Department is attempting to establish a wide-ranging health service. Its achievements have rarely failed to impress visitors, including doctors and other trained medical personnel. At the time of our visit, charts in the Central Hospital showed the Health Department running six regional hospitals, eight health centres, fifteen health stations and over 40 mobile teams. They have trained over 1500 'barefoot doctors', and more than 140 village health workers, as well as traditional midwives and many specialist health personnel.

The EPLF's health strategy has had to confront four main 'constraints': a largely illiterate population with few trained health personnel; the need to involve the population in the delivery of health care; the problems created by the war; lack of resources and the geographical isolation of the EPLF-held areas.

8.1 Health Problems in Rural Eritrea

The pattern of ill-health in Eritrea is typical of a poor Third World country; death and disease have been aggravated by the years of drought and damage from the war. The main health problems result from low standards of nutrition, water supply, sanitation and housing. Malnutrition and anaemia are widespread, decreasing people's resistance to infectious diseases and exacerbating their effect. Malaria, tuberculosis, respiratory infections and intestinal parasites are endemic.

Conditions differ between the lowlands and highlands. The lowland areas are inhabited by pastoral nomads who travel with their herds of camels, cattle, goats and sheep, carrying all their belongings.

Women and children sleep in tents while the men sleep outside, where they are particularly susceptible to malarial mosquitoes. In some lowland areas 80% of the population have malaria. Families and their livestock use the same water sources, often badly contaminated. The staple food is a porridge made from sorghum and salt. A little milk is added by the better off, but vegetables are rarely included. The men eat first; the women and children eat what is left, and when food becomes scarce they are inevitably the first to suffer. Wasted children are a common sight. An EPLF Health Department survey in the eastern lowlands found very high levels of malnutrition, 34% of all children having marasmus (protein and calorie starvation), and 6% kwashiorkor (protein starvation alone). Malnutrition is a factor in most deaths, because it results in common infectious diseases being fatal. In the Barka lowlands, 280 infants per thousand die before their first birthday. Overall, the Health Department estimates that more than half of Eritrean children — 520 per thousand — die before the age of five.

In the highlands, Eritreans live in settled villages of mainly subsistence farmers. Their diet is largely a fermented bread made from local grains. Vegetables and fruit are unavailable except near towns and irrigation schemes. Scurvy and rickets are common. Typhoid and tuberculosis thrive in the cramped conditions of village houses. Sickness makes it harder to cope with the daily physical toil: women have to fetch water from distant wells and haul it up the mountainside. Cultivating the land with primitive tools and hard manual labour raises food needs.

8.2 The Fight against Disease

At the end of the 19th century the Italians introduced a medical service into Eritrea, initially designed purely to protect the settlers from the tropical diseases they encountered. They established a hospital at Asmara, and set up clinics in the areas of Italian settlement. Later, the postwar Labour government during the British occupation opened a network of dispensaries, and although some facilities, such as the hospital at Zula, were dismantled when the British left, Eritrea had a relatively advanced health service by the beginning of the federal period. This initially prospered under Eritrean administration. Mother and child clinics were established and hospitals renovated. But since colonisation, little had been done to teach the rural population about the causes and spread of disease. Sanitation and hygiene were rudimentary.

In the late 1950s Haile Selassie's regime began to cut Eritrea's health budget, which by 1965 had fallen to a third of its 1955 level. As the Eritrean liberation movement became more active, the Ethiopians began to close clinics and destroyed a further sixteen in the fighting of the late 1960s.

In the rural areas, where the limited health services provided by successive colonial authorities had minimal impact, traditional healers were still consulted and commanded much respect. Traditional medicine is often linked to religious beliefs and involves much mystification — merely mentioning the name of a herb is thought to cancel out its effect. This belief in magical cures has influenced the population's attitudes to modern medicine and treatments involving pain, such as injections, are considered particularly efficacious. Common medical practices include herbal medicines made from leaves, roots and barks, as well as the use of holy water and amulets, burning and blood-letting. Surgical operations such as clitoridectomy, infibulation, excision of the uvula, and the cutting of tendons in cases of rheumatism were widespread.

In tackling these problems the EPLF had to face a number of immediate constraints. They lacked trained personnel since the health workers were in the towns controlled by the Ethiopians. They lacked buildings for clinics and hospitals, of which there were none outside the towns. Also, the rural population lived in conditions where ill health was inevitable.

The EPLF set up clinics in the settled areas and served the nomadic zones and the contested areas with mobile teams. The EPLF health service started in 1970 with a single mobile clinic, only competent to treat malaria and give basic first aid. Training of the first group of 25 'barefoot doctors' began in 1972, but it was not until the period 1975 to 1978 that the health service really took off. During these years hundreds of skilled Eritreans, including doctors, nurses and paramedical staff, fled the towns and joined the EPLF. The People's Assemblies then being established in the villages were asked to select candidates for training in the regional hospitals as 'barefoot doctors' and 'barefoot midwives'. The courses were short (3 to 6 months) in order to equip a large number of health workers with essential skills. In 1978 alone, 410 barefoot doctors and 18 barefoot midwives were trained.

The Central Hospital in Sahel province is now the main training hospital for operating theatre assistants, anaesthetists, radiographers, laboratory technicians and pharmacists. It also provides higher medical training for experienced nurses. During our visit to this hospital, we were struck by the commitment of these students, who were to be seen studying everywhere — under trees in the hospital area as well as in the wards or in the library. The more advanced courses are conducted in English so that students can read medical textbooks written in English as well as the more summary manuals provided by the Health Department in Tigrinya. Some highly specialist training is provided by visiting foreign medical teams. This began in November 1980 with an Italian surgical team from Florence, to be followed by teams from Belgium, France, Denmark and Norway.

The EPLF Health Department makes use of two structures to teach the population about the prevention of disease and to improve living conditions at village level — the mobile teams and the health committees of the People's Assemblies. The mobile teams give health lectures in the community following the curriculum drawn up by the Education and Research section of the Health Department, and distribute 'Ray of Health', a quarterly magazine, first produced in 1977, which has proved one of the EPLF's most widely read publications. This deals with a broad range of subjects — the cause, transmission and prevention of diseases, first aid, contraception, latrine construction, hygienic food preparation, the need to get early advice from health workers, and the uses and dangers of traditional medical practices.

The village health committee is given basic training in health education and first aid, and takes responsibility for supervising the cleanliness of the water supply, for digging latrines, for garbage disposal, and for organising 'sanitation days'. Among the tasks of the village education committee is to encourage the population to attend literacy classes which themselves disseminate basic health education messages.

8.3 Involving the People

The success of both the EPLF's social revolution and its military struggle depends not only on gaining and maintaining the support of the Eritrean population but also on securing its active participation. Providing a health service to satisfy the demands of both fighters and civilians is a key feature in the process of revolutionary change in Eritrea.

Until Barka province came under EPLF control, the population served by the Health Department was either fighters, the settled population in contested areas, or the nomadic population of the EPLF's base area in Sahel province. These needs were considered best met by mobile health units, consisting of two barefoot doctors, one responsible for clinical work, the other for health education, a barefoot midwife and two medical assistants. They travel to villages by camel or donkey and occasionally in EPLF vehicles. Difficult cases or those requiring long treatment are referred to permanent health centres. During the drought the mobile health units have been coordinating their visits with ERA's food distribution, thus ensuring access to a much larger share of the vulnerable population.

'Barefoot doctors' are selected by the EPLF Department of Public Administration from candidates proposed by the local committees.

They must be literate, and they receive six months' training in one of the hospitals. This covers anatomy, physiology, biology, pharmacology and sterile technique, followed by two years' field work attached to mobile health units treating civilians or fighters, and finally six months' advanced hospital training in a medical specialisation. Their training therefore involves tackling a range of health problems requiring medical and surgical intervention including prescription of basic drugs, suturing and even amputation, giving health advice and follow-up care. Preventative health is emphasised and barefoot doctors are also teachers of nutrition, hygiene, sanitation and childcare. We saw copies of a monthly bulletin 'Barefoot Doctor' which is produced by the Health Department to keep barefoot doctors up to date and well informed. The barefoot midwife training includes an emphasis on obstetric problems. We met one group of young women, each from a different Eritrean nationality, being trained on the delivery wards of the Central Hospital.

Providing a health service to the nomads clearly involves special difficulties granted that the population is dispersed and often on the move. Mobile health units have provided a partial solution. Nomadic encampments hear of the arrival of a mobile unit in the vicinity and bring in their sick or ask the team to visit them. Otherwise nomadic families must come to the clinics, camping nearby with their livestock. At the time of our visit the clinics were providing food in cases of need, and the health staff were giving health education to nomadic families, while involving them in the care of their sick. In the long term, the Health Department sees the provision of an effective health service to the nomads to be possible only when they choose to settle. Otherwise medical follow-up for re-vaccination or other treatment is difficult or impossible. The EPLF's long-term policy is to persuade the nomads to settle by making the conditions in settled communities sufficiently attractive. However, this approach neglects the important economic role that nomadic grazing will continue to fill on those marginal lands unsuitable for development with improved methods of soil and water conservation.

When the EPLF moved into Barka province in 1981, the Health Department was confronted by the new task of providing a health service to a settled population where military control was no longer contested. The response was to launch the 'Eritrea Public Health Programme' and emphasise the training of two categories of health workers — 'village health workers' and 'traditional midwives'. Trainees are selected directly by the local health committees for their interest in, and knowledge of, the community, its customs and its attitudes towards sickness and healing. Village health workers receive three months' general health training from the EPLF's Department of Public Administration, while traditional midwives receive six months' instruction from the Health Department's gynaecology and obstetrics section. Nearly four out of five village health workers — and all the midwives — are women. Family care during the training period is assumed by the village.

Village health workers not only provide basic health care and health education. They also keep records of health needs and health problems in the community, to be forwarded via the local public health coordinator to the ERA. Complex cases are referred to the nearest clinic or hospital. Traditional midwives are usually older women already confident in their work. On returning to their villages after training, these women continue to do home deliveries, but also hold mother and child health clinics, giving health education and antenatal and postnatal care.

Throughout its history the EPLF Health Department has had to cope with the particularly poor health of Eritrean women, who not only suffer the hazards of childbearing but eat a worse diet, and carry an even heavier workload than their menfolk. In the eastern lowlands, death in childbirth is common. The Director of the Central Hospital showed us a Health Department study which recorded a 27% maternal mortality rate for a limited sample of nomadic women in an area with particularly severe health problems.

This extremely high figure is thought to be partly due to the narrowness of women's pelvises deformed both by (1) rickets in childhood, a result of Vitamin D deficiency, and (2) infibulation, after which the child's legs are bound together for 40 days until the wounds heal. A further reason must be the extreme anaemia of the lowland women due to the lack of iron in the daily sorghum porridge diet. In this condition, resistance to disease is very low and a small amount of blood loss can lead to a state of shock and death.

The Health Department has found it hard to provide a service to these nomadic women. Unless the women attend the clinics or are examined by the 'barefoot midwives', it is impossible to identify which pregnant women are most at risk. A gynaecologist at the Central Hospital told us horrific stories of nomadic women, who, when complications arise in labour, try traditional remedies first and only make the trip to the clinic when these fail. Some patients arrive at the late second stage of labour with the baby's shoulder or limb stuck in the vulva.

Infibulation and Clitoridectomy

Extra complications arise from infibulation and clitoridectomy. In the mainly Muslim lowlands infibulation (the removal and suturing of the labia) of young girls is extensive. In the predominantly Christian highlands the operation is limited to clitoridectomy (the excision of the clitoris). Both operations are done before the girl reaches the age of two. These practices are justified on religious grounds or explained in terms of ensuring virginity before marriage and reducing women's sexual drive to encourage loyalty to her husband. Infibulation and clitoridectomy can lead to bleeding, infection from non-sterile implements, tetanus, urine retention and complications in labour, and are the most dangerous of Eritrean traditional practices.

Attempts in other countries such as Egypt and Sudan to curtail these practices by both legislation and health education have met with many difficulties and very limited success. The EPLF's campaign has by contrast achieved significant results in specific areas. Within the EPLF, nearly a third of whose members are women, the practices have apparently been eliminated. In some areas which the EPLF has been administering for many years — such as in Semhar province, north of Massawa — the practice has been much reduced. The Health Department stresses the health problems of infibulation and clitoridectomy within the context of general health education on a range of different issues.

We were told about the history of the campaign at She'eb, a village through which we passed. The Health Department had been giving health education there in the mid-1970s at a time when the ELF and EPLF were able to enter each other's territories. An EPLF 'barefoot doctor' when explaining the health complications associated with infibulation said the practice was now illegal (the EPLF has not in fact 'banned' it, recognising the problems involved in enforcing such a ban). An ELF cadre began to criticise the EPLF's opposition, saying that inherited traditions should be maintained. Infibulation thereby became a political issue in the community. Those who supported the EPLF stopped it, while those who did not continued the operation. It seems that most women themselves were in favour of stopping the practice.

The Health Department is optimistic that infibulation and clitoridectomy will eventually disappear in the context of wider changes taking place in people's attitudes towards women in Eritrean society — where decisions at village level are taken by committees on which women are now represented, where women are organised in their own association, and where literacy and political education campaigns are taking place. The EPLF plans to wait until the dangers of these practices are generally understood before passing a law banning them.

The success of the EPLF's health service thus has depended on its ability to involve the Eritrean population through the structures which the EPLF has established. As we have seen, local committees at village level select the health recruits for their area, and take responsibility for health education and sanitation. The mass associations are also involved — they provide labour for building the camouflaged buildings of the clinics, funds to purchase medicines, and volunteers to prepare the meals in the hospitals. Health workers in the Ethiopian-controlled towns smuggle out drugs and equipment to the EPLF, and an 'Eritrean Medical Association' has been set up to attract the interest and involvement of the many Eritrean medical personnel working or studying outside Eritrea.

8.4 The Wounded and the War

The EPLF has had to forge its health service while fighting a major war, both while launching attacks and defending itself and its territory against the successive offensives of the Ethiopian army. The war has killed tens of thousands of Eritreans, and left a comparable number of fighters and civilians wounded and needing treatment. To a large extent the warhas determined the nature of the service provided. Mobile health units can move in and out of areas quickly. Health clinics and hospitals are carefully camouflaged to avoid air attack. Particular precautions must be taken in the contested areas beyond the Ethiopian lines.

The EPLF member responsible for the health service in the 'semi-liberated' areas told us that 18 of the 23 EPLF health clinics are sited in such areas, although this number may vary, given the occasional sorties of the Ethiopian army from the towns. When warning is received of the movement of troops towards a particular clinic, it is dismantled and temporarily removed or literally buried underground. The clinics are permanently prepared for this eventuality. We were told in some detail how two days previously he had supervised the 'burying' of the hospital in Serae province. Most of its departments had been built totally underground, and the rooms containing the X-ray equipment, laboratory equipment and medical stores merely had to be sealed and all entrances camouflaged. The whole operation had been completed within 12 hours.

On our visit we were continually meeting injured fighters, some with serious disabilities, who were taking an active part in the economy of the base area. Over 23 years of war, the numbers of Eritreans wounded in the fighting is very high. But it is clearly a tribute to the EPLF's medical services that so many survive and continue to take an active role in the struggle. The EPLF consider the provision of a high standard of health care an essential component of meeting the needs and wishes of the population. In the case of fighters, the high standard of care for the wounded inspires their confidence. Furthermore, for a small population fighting against a numerically much larger force in a protracted war, the saving of lives is imperative.

The Director of the Central Hospital claimed that the Health Department is able to treat 99% of the cases of war injuries. Very few of the injured are treated abroad. Rates of recovery at EPLF facilities are very high — the death rate of the war injured once they arrive at a hospital is 24 per thousand.

The Central Hospital

The Central Hospital is not only the main training hospital but also the main hospital for treating wounded fighters. It has 420 beds and at the time of our visit 70% of these were occupied by wounded EPLF fighters, 15% by wounded Ethiopian prisoners and 15% by civilians. These proportions vary with the level of military activity — our visit came shortly after the extensive battles at Tessenei and Mersa Teklai and on the Nacfa front.

The hospital is spread out over five kilometres of dry mountain valley floor, with wards and departments carefully hidden under trees or built into the hillside. The hospital moved to this site in 1982 after the previous site had been subject to heavy bombardment. We visited operating theatres, surgical, medical, orthopaedic and obstetric wards, a special unit for facial injuries, as well as the laboratories and X-ray units, an opthalmic unit and a dentistry unit. As blood storage facilities are not yet available, the hospital keeps a register of local donors, who can be called upon as the need arises.

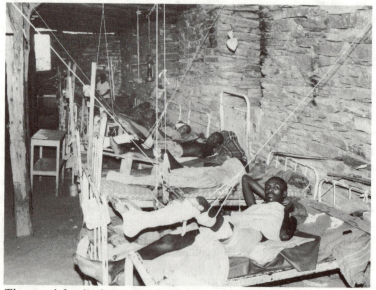

The ward for limb injuries at the Central Hospital.

The ward for patients with facial injuries provided some startling examples of the sophisticated care available. One man had been shot in the face, the bullet entering his cheek and emerging from his neck on the other side; another fighter, a woman, had had one side of her lower jaw completely smashed. Both were well on the road to recovery but unable to speak as their jaws were immobilised by temporary clamps. They were being fed by a tube through the nose.

Another ward contained arm and leg injuries. Sophisticated techniques obviating plaster are being used effectively following a training period by one of the visiting foreign medical teams. In spite of the psychological trauma of serious injury and, in many cases, of amputation, this ward was by no means gloomy. Patients were lively and talked a great deal about the EPLF's recent victories.

The EPLF Health Department also cares for the large numbers of prisoners captured during the fighting. On our visit to the operating theatre, the surgical team were preparing to amputate the leg of a wounded Ethiopian soldier captured on the Nacfa front.

The Port Sudan Clinic

In Port Sudan, well away from the combat zones, fighters and civilians with leg or spinal injuries are given medical and surgical treatment and helped to rehabilitate at the Paraplegic Centre run by the ERA. Training is given to health workers specialising in physiotherapy. But as we saw during our stay, the centre is much more than a specialised teaching hospital. The more educated patients

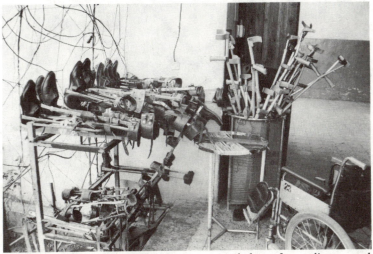

The Paraplegic Centre has its own workshop for calipers and crutches.

Many disabled fighters work in the workshops of the base area.

organise classes to teach their colleagues the higher grades of the school curriculum. Patients learn skills in the workshops of the centre where their own callipers and artificial limbs are made, do the cooking and run the small poultry project which adds eggs and occasionally meat to their diet. We saw the disabled studying their Tigrinya textbooks late into the night. Physiotherapy was imaginative and thorough. Once a week the patients are driven out of town to swim in the Red Sea, and early in the morning the centre reverberates to the shouts of patients playing basketball in their wheelchairs. The patients had formed their own musical bands and were making handicrafts for sale to visitors. Many return to Eritrea to work in the base areas in the workshops or as typists or teachers.

8.5 Medical Supplies: Made in Eritrea

The key constraint on the development of the EPLF's health service is the slim budget within which the Health Department must operate. Supplies of drugs or equipment brought in from outside prove very expensive when transport costs are included. This has forced the Health Department to be inventive with the resources at its disposal within Eritrea and wherever possible to find a 'self-reliant' solution.

As with the workshops described earlier, hospital and clinic

Producing intravenous fluid at the Central Hospital.

buildings and their equipment are made from the available material. The laboratories and intravenous fluid production unit of the Central Hospital were housed in freight transport containers into which windows, doors and ventilation slots had been cut. Cupboards, desks and shelving were made from ammunition boxes. Bomb cases served as stands and the traction rigged up in the orthopaedic wards was a complex system of ropes, beams and sandbags. Even the metal pins used in surgery to unite fractures were made from metal salvaged from captured war material.

The Health Department is now starting to produce its own medical supplies. It has started by producing intravenous fluids, which are expensive to transport because of their weight and bulk. The equipment was bought with funds raised by the Belgian Support Committee, who also sent out a technician to set up the plant and train a qualified Eritrean pharmacist to run it. Sandy, polluted well-water is passed through various stages of filtration, distillation and sterilisation. As we saw, after mixing with salt and sugar it is siphoned into imported bags using aseptic techniques. We were told that continuous operation is currently only meeting half the total needs and a higher capacity distiller is being sought. Intravenous fluid is greatly in demand. It is used for war injuries when fluid cannot be taken orally, for surgical operations that involve high blood loss, and for children and babies with severe dehydration due to diarrhoea.

The equipment needed to set up local production of tablets and capsules of the most frequently used drugs has already arrived in Eritrea and a supply of raw materials donated largely by voluntary agencies in Britain is on its way. The first drugs to be tabletted will be aspirin, tetracycline, sulphonamides, penicillin, chloroquine, vitamin C and the anti-tubercular drug INH. The Health Department estimates that this will save 70% on its current bill for these seven drugs. The urgent need to save scarce resources, the commitment to self-reliance, and not least the absence of competition from multinational or local profit-oriented manufacturers all point to the likely success of this scheme and its future expansion. Having defeated super-power backed armoured divisions in the field, the EPLF is not intimidated by the long arms of the multinational drug companies. The policies of the Health Department are free from the kind of international pressures that the Bangladesh government suffered when it tried to control drug imports in 1982.

The Health Department has also developed a miniature laboratory microscope that is much cheaper and lighter than those currently available. With the help of staff at the London School of Hygiene and Tropical Medicine a model has been produced which is made largely of plastic, is the size of a cigarette packet and costs only £40 — a tenth of the normal price for a microscope. With these, mobile health units will be able to diagnose and prescribe treatment for malaria, TB and intestinal parasites on the spot. The microscopes are also likely to become popular elsewhere in the Third World.

8.6 Implications for the Third World

In the short span of 14 years, the EPLF has made major progress towards establishing a service able to deliver basic health care to a diverse rural population. Its achievements are remarkable, given that the service is developing using minimal resources in an area torn by war. How much can be learned from this experience by other Third World governments?

In many poor Third World countries very few trained health staff operate outside the towns, and their practice is usually limited to dispensing drugs which are expensive and often inappropriate. The preventative aspects of health care seldom go beyond vaccination campaigns. Health education and antenatal care are limited and there are no sanitation campaigns. Aggressive marketing by Western companies of baby foods, sweet soft drinks, and harmful drugs has served to aggravate the situation.

The development of the EPLF's health service has benefitted from three advantages. First, both the health service and Eritrean 'consumers' have been free from commercial pressures which often have such a negative impact on health and health care. Second, the Health Department has had to devise its own solutions to health problems and learn from its mistakes. Third and crucially, apart from a brief period 1977-78, it has had to meet the needs of a rural population without having to satisfy the competing demands for resources and expertise of an urban population. This latter creates a very different dynamic. In other Third World countries,governments are particularly sensitive to pressure from the towns or cities since this is where both the greatest demand and their political support generally lies.

The long-term health of Eritreans depends in part on the further development of the health service, and this needs financial support from outside. The preventative side of this service — sanitation, personal hygiene, health precautions — will need to be increasingly stressed. The acceptance of this approach, which in the longer term will have more effect on people's health, will depend on the confidence health personnel have inspired through a curative service which meets people's more immediate demands.

It it not possible as yet to measure accurately the effect of the EPLF's service on the overall health of the Eritrean people. In a situation of war and drought, assembling the necessary statistics is a secondary priority. It is clear that the shortages of food and water over the last four years have had a devastating impact on the health of the Eritrean population.

Good health in Eritrea will only be achieved when the population has an adequate and varied diet and access to plentiful clean water — as well as basic health services. The end of the current drought will bring immediate improvements. Peace is a precondition for a more secure and productive agriculture, which will have a more lasting impact on health in Eritrea. The pioneering activities of the EPLF, both in health and food production, give grounds for confidence that, with peace and with aid, a highly efficacious programme for the health of the Eritrean people could be rapidly achieved.

CHAPTER 9

Education and Vocational Training

For the EPLF, progressive social change is impossible without a literate and educated population. But the education system it inherited from the colonial era was designed to produce a small educated elite, who used education for their own personal advancement and who despised manual labour. Those Eritreans who did go to school were handicapped in their progress after Amharic was imposed as the medium of instruction.

In formulating its education programmes, the EPLF has had to find ways to provide mass education, to promote the attitude that education should serve the common good, and to raise the status of manual labour. The EPLF also has to determine which languages should be the media of the instruction.

9.1. Education under Colonial Rule

Before the colonial era almost the only education available was religious instruction in churches and mosques: its effect was to reinforce religious and tribal divisions and to inculcate deference and passivity. Mission schools providing a broader education arrived during the nineteenth century, but it was not until the 1920s that the Italians introduced government schooling.

In the next 20 years only 24 primary schools were built. Italian schooling was designed to produce a barely-qualified, deferential labour force and army. Eritreans were not to be allowed to compete for jobs with Italian workers who, in the 1930s, were immigrating in large numbers. Legislation forbade Eritreans from progressing beyond the fourth grade, and teaching stressed the supremacy and glory of Italian culture and history. An Italian Director of Education wrote:

> 'By the end of his fourth year, the Eritrean student should be able to speak our language moderately well; he should know the four arithmetical operations within normal limits; he should be a convinced propagandist of the principles of hygiene; and of history he should know only the names of those who have made Italy great.' (quoted in Trevaskis 1960).

The British put more effort into expanding the education system, and by 1952 there were 100 primary schools, 14 middle schools and 2 secondary schools in Eritrea (Trevaskis 1960). But the British reinforced religious and tribal divisions by segregating schools on religious lines. Muslim schools taught in Arabic, Christian schools in Tigrinya. This policy gave added weight to the Bevin-Sforza plan to partition Eritrea between Arabic-speaking Sudan and Ethiopia, in whose northernmost province, Tigray, Tigrinya is spoken. Under Federation, primary education continued to expand — by 1962, the year of Eritrea's annexation, there were 145 primary schools.

But the increasing intervention of Ethiopia in Eritrean affairs had far-reaching effects on Eritrean schooling. In 1956 Amharic was imposed as the official language and schoolbooks in Arabic and Tigrinya were burnt. Schools were made to inculcate respect and devotion to Ethiopia and its ruler, such as through the compulsory teaching of songs praising the emperor. Schools became centres of political discontent, and from the 1960s were targets of Ethiopian reprisals for guerrilla raids. Many schools were burnt down, particularly in the eastern lowlands, and thousands of schoolchildren and students fled to Sudan as refugees. The military regime which took power in Addis in 1974 inherited responsibility for the urban schools in the areas still under Ethiopian control, but the political repression and terrorisation of the student population of 1977/78 left apathy, fear and resentment in the schools and educational standards plummeted.

9.2. School and Society

In developing its own educational system, the EPLF started from the basic principle that the aim of education must be to reinforce and strengthen the Eritrean revolution. Education must serve the masses is the constant theme of posters and wall paintings in areas controlled by the EPLF. In line with this objective, the EPLF is attempting to link the school to the rest of society, by encouraging community contributions towards building and running schools, and by promoting participation by schoolchildren in the services and production of the village.

Nevertheless, the first educational priority the EPLF set itself was to make every fighter literate — a goal that was achieved by 1972. All new recruits with less than seven years schooling complete their education within the EPLF, and during our visit we often saw fighters sitting in the shade of trees studying. In this respect the EPLA differs from almost every other Third World army. For the EPLF, high levels of literacy and education among the fighters ensure a more effective fighting force, because fighters are highly motivated combatants, not just passive recipients of orders. We were surprised by how well-informed and interested many fighters were about world affairs.

When the EPLF turned its attention to civilian education it was hampered by the unsuitable curriculum inherited from the colonial period and the lack of textbooks in Eritrean languages. The civil war with the ELF delayed the preparation of the EPLF's elementary school curriculum until 1976, when it was introduced experimentally in the newly established 'Revolution School' in the EPLF base area. By 1978 seven grades had been prepared in Tigrinya and Tigre, and the EPLF were teaching some 30,000 students in 150 schools, many in towns captured during the EPLF advance of 1977.

This extraordinary expansion was possible not only because of the efforts of the Education Department, but also because the People's Assemblies and mass organisations built new schools, supplied materials and volunteered teachers. The EPLF withdrew from many of these areas during the retreat of 1978, but a substantial network of EPLF schools now operates clandestinely behind the front lines. The EPLF told us it administers a total of over 100 schools for whom 72 different textbooks are produced, ranging from formal school subjects, to adult literacy, to technical subjects.

One of the tasks of EPLF cadres is to convince poorer peasants of the importance of education. They are often reluctant to send their children to school because they are needed for agricultural and domestic tasks. The EPLF is finding it most difficult to reach the children of nomads, but has set up schools by the main watering

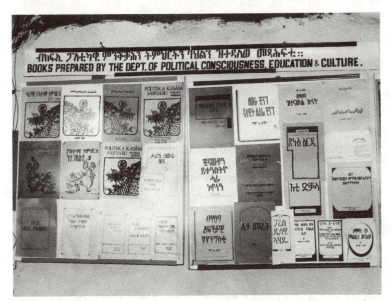

Books are printed in five languages: Tigrinya, Tigre, Afar, Kunama and Arabic.

places where nomad families camp for several weeks at a time.

The education system is designed to encourage young people to participate in the economic and social life of the village. As members of the Red Flowers organisation they help in the local clinic or with cultivating the village communal land. At the time of our visit Revolution School had not reconvened after its holiday break because of a severe shortage of water at the school. Instead, middle and secondary level students had been sent to learn new technical skills in the base area workshops and at the laboratories and wards of the Central Hospital. We met some of them at She'eb and were impressed by their self-assurance and enthusiasm, and by the curiosity they showed towards us.

The EPLF is developing a new culture and art out of the traditions of the different nationalities. Performances by the Red Flowers cultural groups of the dances of Eritrea's nine nationalities stress Eritrean unity and their songs and poems express new revolutionary values. The Red Flowers also perform short plays, illustrating such themes as exploitation by landowners, oppression of women, and the brutality of the occupying regime.

The Revolution School

The Revolution School plays a central role in educational programmes for the EPLF-held areas. It is a boarding school for 2,500 orphans, refugee children and the children of EPLF fighters. Forty per cent of students are girls. From small beginnings in 1976, the school almost doubled after the 'strategic withdrawal', when around a thousand students enrolled after abandoning their former schools in the towns. Like the Central Hospital, classrooms and dormitories are built into the mountain or camouflaged under trees. The Revolution School is the most advanced of the schools — the top class is now doing 9th grade (2nd grade of secondary school) — and acts as a centre for teacher training and for curriculum development. The EPLF claims that the education standards of the school are higher than in Ethiopian government schools and that children joining the Revolution School from those schools have to be put in a class two or three grades below their age-group. Certainly those children we met appeared enthusiastic and well-motivated.

As we saw in Chapter 6, technical training takes place in all the base area workshops where over 3,000 workers have learnt a skill. Science and technology textbooks have been printed in Tigrinya and Tigre — in the Information Department we saw pamphlets on making simple agricultural tools, digging and lining a well, and on the function of pumps and pulleys. The EPLF would like to emphasise practical vocational training at secondary school level, but in spite of international appeals and donations from the National

Union of Eritrean Students in Europe they still lack the necessary laboratory and mechanical equipment.

Near the Revolution School, ERA runs a kindergarten for some 550 three-to-five-year old orphans. At the time of our visit, the kindergarten, like the Revolution School, was very short of water. Diarrhoeal infections and skin problems were on the increase. The staff complained that there was too little water to wash the children's clothes — most of which are ill-fitting donations from Europe or are made in the EPLF's tailoring workshops. The children have hardly any toys or games, but the staff try to keep them occupied and teach them songs and dances. To us, the kindergarten was another example of the EPLF's concern for the casualties of the conflict — and another case of the desperate need for the most basic resources.

Literacy for All

According to the EPLF's National Democratic Programme (see Appendix 2a), literacy is a basic right. Until the 1970s, 80 to 90% of the rural Eritrean population was illiterate, but between 1975 and 1978 the EPLF began the first phase of a literacy campaign. This is still under-way in areas such as Barka province which have recently

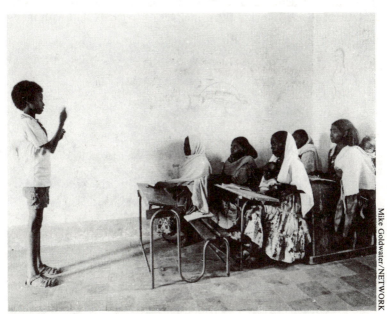

Teenager takes adult literacy class at Aresa, Serae Province.

come under EPLF control, while elsewhere adult education has often moved on to teaching practical subjects like seed treatment, vaccination of livestock, and hygiene in the home. A large number of nomad women have come to the impromptu literacy classes held under trees at watering points. The very fact that they attend public classes, as well as their new ability to read and write, is an important indication of their changing status.

Since the 'strategic withdrawal', the EPLF has concentrated on providing an education for those who fled the towns and became refugees in Sudan. The EPLF set up schools in the refugee camps and in Sudanese towns with a large refugee population. It is essential for the EPLF that the new generation of Eritreans growing up in exile stays in touch with developments in Eritrea, so that these young people are able to reintegrate into Eritrea in the future.

We visited three schools in Port Sudan run by ERA. These schools use the same curriculum as schools inside Eritrea, but with greater emphasis on Arabic so that students can cope better in Sudan and continue with Sudanese education if they have the opportunity. In the evenings the schools are used for adult literacy classes. The teachers are EPLF ex-combatants wounded in the war. School equipment is basic: desks and blackboard are contributed by ERA or by the mass associations in Sudan. The only teaching aids are made by the teachers and children: the classroom walls are lined with colourful sheets showing the principles of hygiene, and with maps

The disabled teach their colleagues at the Port Sudan Paraplegic Centre.

of Eritrea depicting geography, population, resources, clinics and schools. We sat in on a class in the Paraplegic Centre at Port Sudan and watched a wheelchair-bound teacher using empty food tins and a torch to demonstrate an eclipse of the sun.

Given the educational system the EPLF inherited and its own limited resources, the changes we witnessed are remarkable. They are certainly due to the wider changes taking place in Eritrean society. Optimism about the future gives a concrete purpose to education in Eritrea, and motivates all, from the secondary school student learning to dismantle a Land Rover to the nomad woman struggling for the first time with the letters of the alphabet.

PART III

INTERVIEW WITH EPLF
VICE GENERAL SECRETARY

Interview

The authors interviewed Isseyas Aferworki, formerly a member of the General Military Command of the ELF, and a founding member of the EPLF. The interview took place near She'eb in Sahel province, on 21st April 1984 and was tape recorded. These are edited excerpts of the main discussion.

On Non-Alignment and Development

SH: You will be well aware that the Labour Party has published a strong resolution in relation to the whole question of Eritrea, but this is the first time that a representative of the Parliamentary Labour Party has visited the EPLF in the field.* We feel this is overdue, because we have certain debts to clear in relation to the period of British trusteeship after the war.

But we also were persuaded that it was important to see directly what the situation is here and to learn from what you have achieved in the area of development, particularly on the 'basic needs' approach. I think it was Rene Dumont, the French socialist, in his book 'Socialisms and Development' who said 'one working agricultural cooperative is worth five Five-Year paper Plans'.

You not only have pioneered a range of impressive cooperatives but also have prototyped new models of development which frankly are not fully recognised in your statement of objectives. If somebody tried to persuade me of the special merits of the revolution here by showing me your Party's programme, I would regard the emphasis as very centralist. Some people therefore are not sure of the political philosophy of the EPLF, although many of them are beginning to hear of what you are actually doing. It's a kind of socialism by deed, by demonstration, by example, which is beginning to impress people internationally.

IA: The interest you have shown is very encouraging for the EPLF because only a few people have really seen our experience. We feel that the outside world is beginning to understand our situation and is becoming more interested in what we are doing here.

I think the EPLF is an expression of the aspirations of our people.

*The first official representative of the Labour Party was Martin Plaut who represented the Party at the Congresses of Workers and Womens Mass Organisations in December 1982.

We want to transform this society and to have a modern society, not the kind of society we have — people suffering from hunger, people living under very difficult conditions, natural catastrophes, very infertile soil. We have suffered, and 23 years of war in Eritrea has compounded the sufferings of the people. We are striving to fight for our right to self-determination and to transform this society socially, economically, culturally. And to do both at the same time.

One thing special about the EPLF and the Eritrean case is it's a revolution going on in isolation compared with other revolutions in the Third World. For example we have not had the support of the Soviet Union, China and other forces in the world — who gave all kinds of support to the Vietnamese and to other revolutions. Ours is totally different. The Americans are against our cause; the Soviet Union is against our cause — and their global influence influences other forces outside the region. Of course this makes this struggle rely on the resources of the Eritrean people which are very limited. To both fight and socially transform the society is a difficult thing to do without much outside help.

Aid is coming from organisations in Europe, non-governmental organisations cooperating with ERA. We can say that the EPLF relies mainly on the financial support we get from our members outside Eritrea. We cannot say the Eritrean people as a whole contribute because they have been in a very bad economic situation for quite a long time and they need help to keep living. But what we get from outside is very insignificant compared to what we get from the Ethiopian armed forces. We have learned how to rely on ourselves. We now possess practically every sophisticated weapon that the Ethiopian armed forces possess. In fact we can now say we have reached a stage where we can challenge their mechanised units.

SH: You wanted I think to take a non-aligned path, but in the event you have had no choice. Despite difficulties, you have maintained your integrity as a non-aligned movement — unlike some other countries which have been pushed one way or the other in the struggle between the superpowers. Many people in Europe and in Third World countries want non-alignment, but they are not convinced that it is feasible. In Europe, it is evident from the millions of people who have taken to the streets that they want a nuclear-free Europe which is independent of the nuclear policy of either of the superpowers.

In your case you are forced into a policy which seeks to have development independent of either of the superpowers. What you have shown us is a different dynamic, a new development model that supports your non-aligned stance. Your achievements are remarkable — without superpower support — in terms of sophisticated health care provision, in terms not just of repair but the manufacture of equipment like the large-scale machine tools we have seen today, the electrical and electronic work, and other examples.

The military victories are part of the same non-aligned dynamic — they are remarkable by any standards. We have just been with a former Norwegian officer who served with Norwegian troops on United Nations missions in several parts of the world. He says he has never seen such a military success by any Third World country — far less any Third World liberation movement — such as you have just achieved at Mersa Teklai. You mobilised an army in the field and took 7,000 troops by surprise, intercepted them and routed them in a classic defeat.

This has a wider international relevance. In Latin America and Nicaragua, some people ask if it is technically feasible to defeat a force backed by a superpower. What you have done by this battle is not simply regain part of the Sahel province. You have shown the Third World a practical non-alignment in successful armed struggle against forces backed by superpowers.

IA: Militarily we are stronger than some Third World countries; and we are challenging one of the strongest armies in Africa. The mass-media talk about Polisario, about the problem in Chad, but they rarely mention what's happening in Eritrea. The problem is influenced by what the Americans and the Soviet Union want and don't want to be said about Eritrea in the outside world. This is a problem, but we say it's not bad because we might take people by surprise sometime in the future.

People have totally different ideas about the Soviet role in actual confrontations. In Europe they have the experience of Soviet intervention in Eastern Europe. In Europe, people would not believe that a small organisation like the EPLF could challenge the Ethiopian Army and the Soviet advisers. Six years have proved that a small liberation struggle can survive and I think it's a good lesson. For us it's a lesson. We had the determination.

We can now see we are on the offensive. If the situation continues like now we might reach a stage where we will outweigh the Ethiopian armed forces in Eritrea. And the situation will not be reversible as it was in 1977. Then, we fully liberated the countryside but we had to withdraw to the northern part of Eritrea. There was an imbalance of forces. Now that situation would not be repeated because we have a big number of the Soviet weapons in our hands, and we have been able to use them more effectively than the Ethiopian armed forces. They have one superiority we might not be able to match, and that is their air superiority. Now they're mining practically all their defence lines. This has never been done by the Ethiopian armed forces before. It's a sign of their fear that the situation is going against them.

A liberation struggle like ours can challenge with perseverance and determination. But it's not only the combatants that are doing all this. We have our organised departments — the Economic Department, the Public Health Department, the Education Department — fully involved in the social transformation process.

On the Origins of the EPLF

SH: How do you yourselves perceive what you are doing? How do you explain to your own people what you were trying to achieve in terms of the wider debates of socialism in the rest of the world?

IA: One of the biggest problems in the Third World is the division of the society into ethnic, national, religious groupings. No movement in the Third World having this socio-economic formation will ever succeed in achieving anything if it strives to organise itself from religious, tribal and ethnic groupings. That causes divisions and damage and denies any organisation the chance to utilise the potentialities of society.

The ELF's viewpoint about how to organise the struggle against the Ethiopian presence in Eritrea did not start with the concept of organising a nationalist front. The ELF was an alliance of tribal chiefs where a chieftain of a region or someone from that region was given full authority for that region. He would levy taxes, he would punish people, he would do anything to accumulate money and practically do nothing to either educate the population, or alleviate their economic problems.

What people were doing before 1970 was to democratise the nature of the ELF organisation from within, bring new ideas, criticise their practices and try to open dialogue with people at the top, combatants in the rank and file, the population — trying to tell people that this was not the proper way of fighting this war. Unfortunately the ELF leadership resorted to physical liquidation of all the people who were coming with new ideas. This physical liquidation within the ELF intensified the opposition. Finally there was no other choice except to break away from this organisation and found a new organisation which could meet the demands and aspirations of the people. At the beginning you don't conceptualise everything properly. You begin with some concrete experience - our experience was the ELF. Of course outside experience, reading books, learning about other revolutions, does help a lot. But you cannot start from outside. You begin with the situation inside.

On the Soviet Union and the Third World

SH: It must have been a surprise to find that the Soviet Union actually was going to be the superpower opposing your revolution.

IA: We prefer to refrain from entering into big politics, but we are convinced about one thing: the aspiration for socialism in the Third World is completely understandable. There is no other way for Third World societies to transform the social and economic formations of their societies except by following the general socialist trend. As to the details and the models, well we do not have models practically. We need not expect much from the Soviet Union because it was not only after the Derg came to power that the Soviet Union fully stood on the side of the Ethiopian government. They were friends with Haile Selassie and they never openly supported the Eritrean struggle during Haile Selassie's rule. One cannot even say they were sympathetic indirectly. On the other hand, regimes in the region like South Yemen, the liberation movements, and political parties in the Middle East in general who had good relations with the Soviet Union were supporting the Eritrean struggle. The Soviet experience with China, their experience with their friends, not only liberation movements, was already a lesson to the EPLF before they established good relations with the Ethiopian regime. We never took them for enemies, but nor did we have any illusions about their global strategy.

But when the Soviet involvement was escalating to the extent that they were physically involved in the liquidation of our population, well nobody would have found any justification for that. We were contacting them, we were trying to explain matters to them, to at least neutralise their position, to help them look into the situation from the perspective of a genuine interest of the peoples of Ethiopia and Eritrea. But that was ignored and their superpower politics and their strategy was given priority. In the course of six years we now have established one factor which was not established before 1977, that the Soviet Union cannot be a genuine friend to Third World people outside its global interests.

For the Third World, for liberation movements like us, it's very important that people do not come out with ambitious programmes. Economic, social, cultural and other programmes should be modest enough to enable the struggles to maintain their balance, and to be non-aligned, practical. When the Soviet Union was on the side of the Derg, people were saying that it's better now for you to approach the Americans and get their aid. Some progressive political organisations in the region were telling us that we would finally go into the reactionary camp. But we learnt from our experience that our programmes of self-reliance, if fully or practically implemented, would open the way to becoming really non-aligned and independent.

So this experience with the Soviet Union had its implications in our future programmes. If we succeed in achieving or implementing our development projects side by side with our military achievements, then we can really transform this society into a society without over-ambitious projects, whether agricultural, economic, health or others. We can gradually and without haste implement programmes that come from the population and go back to the population, without fully relying on outside help. I think what we are doing now is a prototype of a small experiment of our forthcoming programmes and it's been successful so far.

On Achieving an Independent Autonomous Socialism

SH: You are really now way in advance of your first programme. The challenge of your model of development is remarkably exciting, simply because you have been able to achieve so much with so little.

Take the question of technology transfer between developed and less developed countries. Can one break through the dependency cycle? How can one escape being a dependent under-developed country producing primary commodities for consumption by the global metropolis? You have done this very well. You take a piece of machinery and simply reproduce it in your own workshops; you take a technology and adapt it to your own circumstances. You now have highly sophisticated methods for coping with multiple fractures. Doctors from abroad come in and are with you for a month only, but you are skilled enough to be able to take up these techniques immediately and apply them. You are about to produce your own drugs from their basic components. There are many Third World countries which not only feel they cannot beat a sophisticated army backed by a superpower in the field. They also feel they cannot even beat a multinational drug company.

So while it is impressive that your socialism is still a barefoot socialism, you nonetheless are achieving something which actually has global significance. That you are actually producing sanitary protection is in a way a physical basis of the liberation of women, but it's also a fantastic cultural challenge. You relate to the nomads and their needs not as an enemy to their culture but as sympathisers and friends. You have leapt cultural chasms rather than crept in a gradualist way. What you are doing is bound to be a model to others with similar struggles elsewhere.

But are you really telling us that in your own discussions with each other you are simply pursuing a practical socialism and that you never refer to the debate of the issues which happen elsewhere, to what happened elsewhere in the history of these struggles?

IA: We have our political programmes. We are raising the level of consciousness of the combatants and the members in general along the socialist line and we have our theoretical programmes. We discuss practically every thing, every experience, current events included. We have different types of political programmes, we have seminars organised on zonal levels, political education going to the level of platoons and squads in our army. But what you find in many political organisations is too much stress on theory, creating differences without fully grasping the depth of a certain knowledge, taking stands, accusing each other, antagonising relations to the extent that sometimes you forget what you are fighting for. And externally you go into conflict.

For example, take the Palestinian question. We have our programmes within the rank and file, political programmes based on monitoring radio transmissions from different stations in the Middle East and discussions on the situation of current events. Magazines, books are even taken as materials for discussion but we can never say we side with Arafat or we side with the other factions because such and such position of a certain group is correct and that one is not correct. We are challenged to take positions, to either side with one group or another, but we refrain from that kind of indulgence.

People try to talk about our philosophy, the trend we take, what type of socialism we are trying to establish in Eritrea. Discussing these matters at different levels is a day-to-day affair to the EPLF. We never avoid an issue which has to be discussed — not only in relation to the Eritrean struggle but to the situation in the whole area and to global politics.

From our experience, we have certain critical attitudes to experiences in the Third World. With the present political situation we feel that the Third World and people in this area in particular have to come out with a philosophy that conforms with the present situation and the future developments that might come without the presence of the Soviet Union or the Americans in this region. In the Middle East we now see fundamentalist movements replacing progressive movements. One of the factors for their liquidation was their alignment with the Soviet Union and their consequent misconception of the nature of the struggle they should wage to mobilise the population for a continuous struggle to transform their society. Now they are reconsidering their experience.

Theories should not be taken as they are. Theories in the 20th century after 1917, and from the decolonisation period in the 60s, and from what came after that in the Third World, have to be seriously studied. But Third World societies should come out with new theories about their socialist transformation. They have to work out a programme which would be fully independent from the guidance and the intervention of outside sympathisers like the Soviet Union. They must rely on their own resources and do as much as possible to mobilise the majority of the population.

SH: You want an independent autonomous socialism. You do not want dependence on superpowers. Yet how are you going to get the hundreds of tractors and the other commodities you need? How are you going to convince others without being more specific about your revolution using the language of international socialism? Since not everyone can come here and see it, it is not easy for people to judge your achievements. You run the risk that they may simply postpone their judgement on the Eritrean revolution.

In the short term how do you mobilise international pressure for world public opinion to say it is a scandal that you are one of the major drought areas of the world yet receive no official drought relief, it is a scandal that you are one of the few social groupings in the world which actually can deliver results yet you are not getting the appropriate kind of aid to develop the agriculture, to diversify the diet, to achieve an acceptable nutritional standard?

IA: We might not need big aid from super-powers to implement projects. We can strengthen our relations with countries that could provide us with very simple implements. We have workshops for making spare parts for trucks, our tanks, artillery, everything. We make about 80% of the spare parts we need. But the war is consuming these resources. If we didn't have this war and had more aid we could then utilise our manpower resources, and the simple implements and machinery we get from modest friends. We can I think gradually improve the capacity of the society to be more independent in many fields of development projects. Take tractors for example. We now have in the Department of Transport a section for assembling trucks. There are links between the organisation and some factories in Italy. We buy some of the components of the machinery we cannot manufacture by ourselves. We have the Construction Department, they have their projects of constructing small dams in some parts of our country. What we need is the material for constructing these dams. If we can implement these projects, we can transform agricultural production to provide the raw material for improving the other industrial aspects of development.

I think there is the capacity in Europe, without our going to the Soviet Union or the United States. A simple example: we do not have a textile factory. We have practically all the workers who have been working in the Baratollo textile factory. They can make all sorts of fabrics. Some used to be exported to the region outside Eritrea. What can we do with these skilled people? Can we get the machinery to have a textile factory? We don't need to train people, we have already a big number of skilled workers. We are looking for small machines to at least keep the production going at very low levels. And projects like this might not need very huge sums of money to be invested in order to at least meet the demands of our population. These small scale industries and projects can be implemented without relying on aid from one of the superpowers.

SH: The reason I'm enthusiastic about what you're achieving is that I see what other people are not achieving. So investment in your revolution in my view is justified because one is reinforcing and promoting success. We are disposed to do that not because we feel we should help the successful or that the strong should help the strong but that the Third World desperately needs this model of success, and that it has to be supported.

On Military Developments

JF: We've heard you've scored certain victories recently at Tessenai, Mersa Teklai, and on the Nacfa front. How do you feel the situation is developing militarily? You mentioned earlier that you felt that the balance was changing, so how do you see the immediate future on the military side and how will this develop in the longer term?

IA: At the moment we are entering a new stage. The past 6 years have been years of consolidating our defence lines and the periphery of our base area. We have nearly finished that stage now. For more than 6 offensives, we were totally on the defensive. Now the initiative is in our hands, we are taking the offensive with Tessenai, Mersa Teklai and the recent attacks we made in the Halhal and Nacfa fronts. We will not give them the chance to regain the superiority they had in the past 5 years.

When it comes to their manpower, after the declaration of the national military service the Derg has not been able to mobilise more than tens of thousands. It's becoming a very difficult political problem for them. People are running away from their home villages, they're not prepared even to come to any kind of compromise with the regime. This is badly affecting their military situation.

As for armaments, one superiority they had was that we never had the capacity to enter into an open area combat. Now we have that capacity. Our mechanisation has improved a lot. What we have captured in the two battles — especially in Mersa Teklai has radically changed the situation. In the past we were on the defensive and their mechanisation was the real threat to us. So we had to keep our positions in very broken areas, mountainous areas. Now it's very easy to fight in open plains. Before their Soviet advisers told them: 'They have finished their hand grenades. They're using dummy bombs to demoralise the army.' Now they really know that we have enough supplies of ammunition. This will have its effect on their way of thinking.

In the past any operation was limited by the logistics of supply — now we don't have that problem. And since they are the source of our supplies they know very well that we have the means. We can say we are in a position to take any action any time, but of course to engage our army in a full-scale offensive or counter-offensive in the positional defence lines we need some time to do the necessary preparations. Eventually they will be driven back from their present positions. They are now realising this fact. So what will happen in the near future will have its political implications, it will not only be a military problem. If they are driven back from their present positions they will never have the capacity to defend the big cities.

In the past 6 offensives, in every offensive we were capturing 5,000, 7,000, 10,000 light arms. We didn't have the manpower to pick up all these arms. Now we are organising our militias, our regional armies, we are better organised, better equipped with new weapons. The possibility exists of defending the whole countryside. Our regional units and the militias which were purely defending their villages, their regions, are now participating in major offensives. The political preparation is more important: militarily we don't see any difficulty facing us to make more advances.

On the Situation in Ethiopia

JF: Can you comment specifically on an item we heard in the news in Britain last month that the Cubans are reducing their troops in Ethiopia?

IA: The Cubans are not leaving. They have decreased the number by one motorised brigade. The Cubans have been clear in many things. It is said that they refused to participate in the war in Eritrea and they have been consistent in that policy. During the 6th offensive, the regime requested that the Cuban units in the Ogaden come to the north to participate in the offensive. But it is said that they refused. The presence of Cuban troops in the Ogaden, however, allows the Ethiopian regime to redeploy and concentrate its forces for its war in Eritrea or aggression against Somalia.

The Cuban problem with the Soviet Union is they are at the gate of the United States and for them to be independent is a difficult matter. They have to come to some kind of concessions with the Soviet Union. But it's very clear that they are not in full agreement with the Soviets on many issues even inside Ethiopia. When the regime was liquidating leftist groups under the name of 'Red Terror' they were reportedly against that policy of the regime. It is also said that the Cubans are not in favour of a military solution in Eritrea.

JF: Do they support your proposal for a referendum?

IA: According to some reports, they do support that proposal, but not officially. Officially it would cause a lot of trouble for them with the Soviet Union. One can understand it from their way of putting things. 'Well, we are with the just cause of the Eritreans and we know that they are doing well but there is nothing we can do.'

That is their position regarding the Eritrean war.

JF: What about the other internal developments inside Ethiopia — particularly the growing strength of some liberation fronts?

IA: There are many political issues which should be resolved before seeing these liberation movements becoming effective towards changing the whole situation in Ethiopia. We have been in a continuous dialogue with these organisations. They must have a common political programme, a viewpoint on what type of government they would establish. What would be the relationship of the autonomous administrative areas they want to establish through the struggle of different nationalities? The multinational organisations like the EPRP, ME'ISON and the present EPDM* and other organisations — what will be the relation of these political parties who are now operating at the level of fronts? How do they visualise their future government, the central government, the autonomous governments? It's a question of policies regarding finance, economy, defence, foreign relations and other issues. Every organisation is having its limited programme and spontaneously operating to liberate a certain area with different military strategies. Plans should be united, you can't have diversified strategies to topple a regime. And they have border problems — one nationality claims that its border is from this area to that area, but another nationality does not accept this. There are also deeply-rooted political problems which have not been resolved. Of course the TPLF* has made much progress.

JF: What will be the effect inside Ethiopia of the EPLF victories?

IA: We now have 14 of the 21 Ethiopian divisions in Eritrea and these are the most advanced units. If we can rout this army it will have its impact inside Ethiopia: it will not be limited to Eritrea. But this would mean a prepared political force to utilise it for a genuine transformation inside the country. The problem of 1974 was that it created a vacuum. There was only the army to fill that vacuum and the consequence of that problem is what's now happening inside Ethiopia politically. Even though we don't give much credit to our achievements in this regard, we can help to a certain degree to bring socialism inside Ethiopia by our efforts to unite our action practically with other liberation movements. You have the Western Somali Liberation Front, the Afar movement, the Oromos, the TPLF, the EPDM. But there are other political forces supported by the Americans now organising themselves in the Sudan like the EPDA, the EDU* and many other smaller organisations. Those organisations who claim to be more democratic and genuine should join hands to unite their action.

*see Glossary

JF: You're saying that in the situation of 1974 there was a vacuum of alternatives, there was a vacuum of power, there didn't exist a coherent opposition at that time. Aren't you also saying that's still really the situation now? So what do you think would happen in practical terms in Ethiopia if the EPLF were to regain Eritrea?

IA: One of the possibilities is of course that the regime will never recognise our achievements. Even liberating Asmara might not be recognised by the regime. They will go on pursuing a military solution. This situation could be really exploited by liberation movements inside Ethiopia, but they don't have the capacity at the moment. But our operations will not be limited to this point. There are many things to be done to topple the regime. We will not be limited to operations within the Eritrean borders. We could have the supply lines of the whole of Ethiopia under the control of the EPLF — the Assab-Asmara-Addis road, and of course the port of Massawa. And then there is the possibility of inflicting losses on their supply line from Djibouti to Addis. This will definitely have its impact on the regime.

But whether it would be wise for us to take such an action is something we have to seriously consider before any move. We are not interested in creating a vacuum in Ethiopia, which would be of great harm to the Ethiopian population and to the situation in the region as a whole. But definitely what we can do here will affect the situation.

JF: If there were further changes to your advantage in the military situation inside Eritrea, and Ethiopia agreed to cease hostilities against Eritrea, agreed to your demands, what would then be your position?

IA: That will be a different question. We have this referendum proposal. We can allow them an outlet to the sea. We can establish relations, not in particular with the present regime, but economic, social, cultural and other ties with a genuine government that does represent the Ethiopian population.

If they are prepared to negotiate and accept our referendum proposals the whole problem would be resolved. That might not mean that we directly negotiate with the present regime. There are demands we have regarding the situation in Ethiopia. In order to have the guarantee of avoiding any eventual conflict between Eritrea and Ethiopia there should be a democratic transformation inside Ethiopia politically. The issue of nationalities and other political problems should be resolved before there can be a durable peace with any government that took power in Addis.

But the options are open of course and if there is no hostility from them then we would not be interested in opening new areas of conflict. What we would strive to do would be to recover what we have lost in 25 years of catastrophic war which has destroyed many things in this society. And it would be to the interest of the Eritrean people in the first place to end the hostility with the regime in Addis Ababa in a way that would be acceptable to the other side.

On the Other Eritrean fronts

JF: We heard in London that there are talks now between the EPLF and the ELF-PLF. How are they progressing? And what's happened to the Jeddah agreement between the other Eritrean fronts?

IA: When it comes to the ELF-PLF it has practically nothing inside Eritrea. It is a one-man show. Nevertheless, we are trying to maintain contacts with all the Eritrean groups.

The problem with the other Eritrean organisations is that it's very difficult to talk about organisations. One organisation can have about 1,000 full-time diplomats outside, but nobody in Eritrea. That is an organisation. Their efforts are aimed at maintaining and keeping their financial capacity to finance their bureaucrats. One thing we propose: let's coordinate our action, let's collect all our money and use it for the struggle. This is a simple proposal. They rejected it. Where can we cooperate unless we practically channel all our resources to the benefit of the population? And every regime tries to find a group that can be used at the moment and in the future for their own national tactics in this area. We are not prepared to serve strategies of neighbouring countries in the area.

The problem with the Saudis (who sponsored the Jeddah agreement) is that they are in full contradiction with the aspirations of our society. The Saudis' strategy is to use the Eritrean struggle as an external buffer area for balancing, creating pressures here and there to influence the situation in the Horn as a whole and Ethiopia in particular. For them Eritrea is an instrument. Theirs is not a genuine interest in supporting the self-determination of the Eritrean people. For that matter they don't want an independent organisation to survive inside Eritrea.

Of course we are not a kingdom, we are not struggling to establish a government like theirs. We have openly told them that we are socialist and our line is very clear. And we are independent, we don't ally ourselves with any power within this region. They consider the EPLF a threat because if the EPLF succeeds, the Eritrean card will not be in their hands. So they have to create organisations and support other groups outside the EPLF.

Their Jeddah agreement and the machinations behind that unity were to achieve discord. These small groups which were outside Eritrea had to be reorganised to challenge the EPLF. They did not succeed of course. A lot of money was put into that project. There was a plan of recruiting tens of thousands of people from the refugees in the Sudan to establish them. The Saudis of course assumed it's very easy: if you have money you can buy people from the streets and establish an army to challenge the EPLF. Of course that failed, and now they seem to be discouraged about their projects, but their attitude to the Eritrean problem and the EPLF in particular is very clear.

JF: Finally, there's also been talk recently of right-wing Conservative MPs in Britain such as Winston Churchill and Julian Amery speaking for the Eritrean case. What is your attitude to this?

IA: The support coming from the Right in Europe can be related to a situation in Europe. The assumption that the regime in Addis could ever be detached from the Soviet Union and that they could replace the Soviet Union, is fading away. In the past there was not even an interest in what was happening in Eritrea. The assumption was that one day in the future the experience of Egypt might repeat itself in Ethiopia. Now that belief, or that expectation is fading away.

An interest in the Eritrean case is growing in Europe in general. But one has to find out more about this interest before evaluating or saying that it's for this intention or for that intention. Labour and socialist parties have had a long contact with us and they have been genuine and clear about their position. As for Conservative parties to be interested at the moment, there must be some motivation for their interest — maybe the Soviet factor. The parties of the Right are now manoeuvering with certain bankrupt groups, trying to give them more publicity in the British news media. Once the Right have confirmed that it's no use manoeuvering or flirting with the regime in Addis in order to detach it from the Soviet Union, they have to decide whether to support the Eritrean movement as an instrument for pressurising or changing the whole situation to their interest. They might try to use someone to that end. But we would not be misled by any support that comes to the Eritrean struggle if it's aimed at manipulating the situation for interests that do not conform with the aspirations of our population.

Summary Conclusions

1 The Case for Self-determination

1.1 Eritrea was established as a distinct entity when the Italians occupied the territory in 1889. The experience of 60 years of colonial rule under the Italians and the British gave the Eritrean people an identity distinct from the Ethiopian people.

1.2 The decision of the UN in 1950 to federate Eritrea with Ethiopia (itself unsatisfactory and controversial) was abrogated by Ethiopia's illegal annexation of Eritrea in 1962. Eritrean parties and trade unions were banned, the Ethiopian language Amharic imposed in schools and in any official communication, Eritrean industry partially dismantled and moved to Ethiopia, and the population of both the towns and the rural areas intimidated.

1.3 Twenty-three years of military opposition to Ethiopian rule by the Eritrean liberation fronts and the support the EPLF receives from the population in the 85% of Eritrea which it now administers, is a clear indication of the extent to which Ethiopian rule is not accepted.

1.4 Britain administered Eritrea during the period 1941 to 1952 when the future of Eritrea was being decided, and has a particular responsibility, both directly and indirectly through institutions such as the EEC, in helping find a solution to the Eritrean conflict which reflects the wishes of the Eritrean people.

1.5 The war has resulted in the death and disablement of tens of thousands of Eritreans and Ethiopians. It has led to the displacement of at least half a million people within Eritrea and the flight of nearly a third of a million refugees. In Eritrea, the war has devastated the economy and frustrated the implementation of programmes which can bring food and water to all. In Ethiopia, the war has meant the compulsory recruitment of its youth into the army and the spending of around 30% of its GNP on its armed forces, while the government itself estimates that four million people face famine in 1984. It is imperative that a peaceful solution is found in order to end this suffering.

1.6 The military support provided to Ethiopia first by the US and Israel, and now by the Soviet Union and its allies has led to the militarisation of the region and is the reason why the Eritrean war has lasted so long. The EPLF is arming itself massively with the weapons it captures. The military defeat of the Eritrean resistance seems impossible. The war will only end through a negotiated political solution based on self-determination.

1.7 The wide ranging successes of the EPLF in building up transport, light industry, health and education — and the agricultural and mineral potential of Eritrea — indicated not only that future economic viability is possible, but also that the EPLF has prototyped remarkable models of self-governing development.

2 The EPLF as a Political Force

2.1 The EPLF is now the single liberation front of any significance operating in Eritrea. It fully controls about 35% of the land area of Eritrea. A further 50% is administered by the EPLF while being open to temporary Ethiopian military re-occupation.

2.2 The military strength of the EPLF is now considerable. Its recent victories involved the capture of large supplies of arms and ammunition, including tanks and anti-aircraft guns. It now can field not only a guerrilla army, but also a 'regular' army able to fight and win outright conventional pitched battles against a Soviet-backed Ethiopian army. The war is entering a new phase, distinct from the military stalemate that characterised the period 1979 to 1983.

2.3 The EPLF maintains a position of non-alignment in international affairs. The abandoning by the Soviet Union of their support for Eritrea's independence in favour of an alliance with Ethiopia has neither resulted in the EPLF turning to the USA, nor in the EPLF changing its commitment to socialist transformation in Eritrea.

3 Economy, Society and Aid

3.1 The EPLF has carried out a number of reforms which have radically altered the balance of local power towards the poorer sections of the peasantry, the landless and women, particularly in the areas it has administered for many years. These have been carried through by organising the disadvantaged population into associations of poor peasants and women. The most notable reforms are the redistribution of land and major steps towards women's liberation from the bonds of feudal society.

3.2 The EPLF is implementing a 'self-reliant' development strategy, in which the front itself manufactures machines, tools and spare parts wherever possible, and in which it stresses the training and education of Eritreans. The EPLF has gone a long way to meeting the basic needs of the population — in particular in setting up a wide-reaching and effective health service, plus basic education in Tigrinya and Tigre and adult literacy in local languages.

3.3 The long-term development assistance currently being received by the EPLF Departments is very limited. It comes mainly from

Western voluntary organisations and from the fundraising efforts of the Eritrean refugee population's own organisations.

3.4 The need for long-term assistance programmes is vast, and structures and skilled personnel exist for their implementation. Priority areas are agricultural reconstruction, well-digging, re-afforestation, transport, and the establishment of local production of agricultural tools, essential drugs and clothes. Because of the EPLF's social and economic policies the main beneficiaries of such programmes will be the poorest and most needy Eritreans.

4 The Food Crisis and Emergency Aid

4.1 The drought in Eritrea, now in its fourth consecutive year, has led to severe shortages of food and water in most areas of Eritrea. In many areas wells are dry and people are abandoning their homes in search of food. Mortality rates are rising. A high proportion of livestock has already died. ERA's estimate that 1.2 million people in EPLF-administered areas need emergency food assistance is supported by all independent observers who have visited Eritrea.

4.2 The war is a major cause of the food shortages. The Ethiopian armed forces have confiscated and destroyed crops, mined fields, and bombed livestock.

4.3 The vast majority of Eritreans affected by the drought are in the areas under EPLF administration. Only a small proportion of these will get food from the Ethiopian government distribution points in the towns. The rest must be reached by ERA who have established a distribution network for emergency supplies. ERA has at its disposal a fleet of trucks with highly organised workshops for their service and repair, a network of fuel stations, and large numbers of staff and volunteers. Elected village committees have identified the most needy in the communities. Their data is coordinated by ERA to ensure the optimum use of any assistance.

4.4 A mere 2% of ERA's estimated needs for emergency assistance in 1984 had been covered by May. The total contribution of governmental and international agencies is meagre and miniscule in relation to the need.

4.5 The isolation of the drought areas and the further difficulties of visiting a country in a state of war, have meant that media coverage of the drought and war has been scant, leading to a situation where there is little international awareness and concern for the suffering of the Eritrean people.

Recommendations

1 The Aid Agencies (governmental and non-governmental)

● To urgently consider either starting or increasing aid to ERA to provide relief assistance to the population in need (and particularly to the population already displaced).

● Assistance should either be in kind (grain, cooking oil, medicines, shelter, trucks) or in financial contributions to enable ERA to make purchases in Sudan and to pay the transport costs of the relief operation.

● Assistance should be urgently considered by international agencies for the approximately 7,000 Ethiopian prisoners of war held by the EPLF, which currently provides for their needs in food, shelter and medical care at the cost of other local services.

2 The Labour Party

● To mobilise support for the 1982 Conference resolution which supported both the Eritrean case for national self-determination and the EPLF's proposals for an internally supervised referendum on the future of Eritrea.

● To reaffirm the commitment in its 1982 resolution to provide when next in government direct financial and material support to the EPLF and ERA, and to seek from the EPLF and ERA before the next British general election an outline proposal for a 'package of aid for national reconstruction and development' in six major sectors of the Eritrean economy, which will form the basis of aid to be provided by the next Labour government.

● To encourage the definition of the support for the Eritrean case expressed by other socialist parties and groupings such as the Socialist International and the Confederation of Socialist Parties of the European Community into active support for the referendum proposal; and to encourage socialist parties which have yet to take a position to endorse the need for such a referendum.

● To welcome, and support through its MEPs, the European Parliament resolution of 12th April 1984 which 'strongly urges the Ethiopian government to find a peaceful and negotiated solution of the conflict between it and the Eritrean peoples, which takes account of their identity, as recognised by the United Nations resolution of 2 December 1950, and is consistent with the basic principles of the OAU'.

● To encourage the countries of the European Economic Community and of the Council of Europe to follow up on the resolution of the European Parliament by raising the issue of Eritrea at the United Nations.

● To monitor the European Commission's response to the European Parliament's resolution of 12th April 1984 which (a) 'calls on the Commission to maintain and increase its food aid... for the peoples of Eritrea... being severely affected not only by drought and famine, but also by military conflict, and to ensure that the means of its distribution are improved' and (b) 'asks the Commission of the European Communities to take all necessary steps to ensure that the humanitarian aid granted reaches all the people affected, irrespective of their political sympathies'

● To strongly discourage any participation by the European Commission in programmes initiated by the Ethiopian government and/or UNHCR which encourage the repatriation of Eritrean or Ethiopian refugees from Sudan or Djibouti, if there exists any suspicion that the refugees may not be returning voluntarily or that they do not have full and accurate information about the prevailing conditions in the areas of Ethiopia to which they may be going.

Documents

APPENDIX 1

The 1950 UN Resolution on Eritrea

Resolution 390 (V), 'Eritrea: Report of the United Nations Commission for Eritrea; Report of the Interim Committee of the General Assembly on the Report of the United Nations Commission for Eritrea,' from the Fifth United Nations General Assembly, 316th Plenary Meeting, 2 December 1950.

Whereas by paragraph 3 of Annex XI to the Treaty of Peace with Italy, 1947, the Powers concerned have agreed to accept the recommendation of the General Assembly on the disposal of the former Italian colonies in Africa and to take appropriate measures for giving effect to it,

Whereas by paragraph 2 of the aforesaid Annex XI such disposal is to be made in the light of the wishes and welfare of the inhabitants and the interests of peace and security, taking into consideration the views of interested governments,

Now therefore

The General Assembly, in the light of the reports of the United Nations Commission for Eritrea and of the Interim Committee, and

Taking into consideration

(a) The wishes and welfare of the inhabitants of Eritrea, including the views of the various racial, religious and political groups of the provinces of the territory and the capacity of the people for self-government,

(b) The interests of peace and security in East Africa,

(c) The rights and claims of Ethiopia based on geographical, historical, ethnic or economic reasons, including in particular Ethiopia's legitimate need for adequate access to the sea,

Taking into account the importance of assuring the continuing collaboration of the foreign communities in the economic development of Eritrea,

Recognizing that the disposal of Eritrea should be based on its close political and economic association with Ethiopia, and

Desiring that this association assure the inhabitants of Eritrea the fullest respect and safeguards for their institutions, traditions, religions and languages, as well as the widest possible measure of self-government, while at the same time respecting the Constitution, institutions, traditions and the international status and identity of the Empire of Ethiopia,

A. Recommends that:

1. Eritrea shall constitute an autonomous unit federated with Ethiopia under the sovereignty of the Ethiopian Crown.

2. The Eritrean Government shall possess legislative, executive and judicial powers in the field of domestic affairs.

3. The jurisdiction of the Federal Government shall extend to the following matters: defence, foreign affairs, currency and finance, foreign and interstate commerce and external and insterstate communications, including ports. The Federal Government shall have the power to maintain the integrity of the Federation, and shall have the right to impose uniform taxes throughout the Federation to meet the expenses of federal functions and services, it being understood that the assessment and the collection of such taxes in Eritrea are to be delegated to the Eritrean Government, and provided that Eritrea shall bear only its just and equitable share of these expenses. The jurisdiction of the Eritrean Government shall extend to all matters not vested in the Federal Government, including the power to maintain the internal police, to levy taxes to meet the expenses of domestic functions and services, and to adopt its own budget.

4. The area of the Federation shall constitute a single area for customs purposes, and there shall be no barriers to the free movement of goods and persons within the area. Customs duties on goods entering or leaving the Federation which have their final destination or origin in Eritrea shall be assigned to Eritrea.

5. An Imperial Federal Council composed of equal numbers of Ethiopian and Eritrean representatives shall meet at least once a year and shall advise upon the common affairs of the Federation referred to in paragraph 3 above. The citizens of Eritrea shall participate in the executive and judicial branches, and shall be represented in the legislative branch, of the Federal Government, in accordance with law and in the proportion that the population of Eritrea bears to the population of the Federation.

6. A single nationality shall prevail throughout the Federation:

(a) All inhabitants of Eritrea, except persons possessing foreign nationality, shall be nationals of the Federation;

(b) All inhabitants born in Eritrea and having at least one indigenous parent or grandparent shall also be nationals of the Federation. Such persons, if in possession of a foreign nationality, shall, within six months of the coming into force of the Eritrean Constitution, be free to opt to renounce the nationality of the Federation and retain such foreign nationality. In the event that they do not so opt, they shall thereupon lose such foreign nationality;

(c) The qualifications of persons acquiring the nationality of the Federation under sub-paragraphs (a) and (b) above for exercising their rights as citizens of Eritrea shall be determined by the Constitution and laws on Eritrea;

(d) All persons possessing foreign nationality who have resided in Eritrea for ten years prior to the date of the adoption of the present resolution shall have the right, without further requirements of residence, to apply for the nationality of the Federation in accordance with federal laws. Such persons who do not thus acquire the nationality of the Federation shall be permitted to reside in and engage in peaceful and lawful pursuits in Eritrea;

The rights and interests of foreign nationals resident in Eritrea shall be guaranteed in accordance with the provisions of paragraph 7.

7. The Federal Government, as well as Eritrea, shall ensure to residents in Eritrea, without distinction of nationality, race, sex, language or religion, the enjoyment of human rights and fundamental liberties, including the following:

(a) The right to equality before the law. No discrimination shall be made against foreign enterprises in existence in Eritrea engaged in industrial, commercial, agricultural, artisan, educational or charitable activities, nor against banking institutions and insurance companies operating in Eritrea;

(b) The right to life, liberty and security of person;

(c) The right to own and dispose of property. No one shall be deprived of property, including contractual rights, without due process of law and without payment of just and effective compensation;

(d) The right to freedom of opinion and expression and the right of adopting and practising any creed or religion;

(e) The right to education;

(f) The right to freedom of peaceful assembly and association;

(g) The right to inviolability of correspondence and domicile, subject to the requirements of the law;

(h) The right to exercise any profession subject to the requirements of the law;

(i) No one shall be subject to arrest or detention without an order of a competent authority, except in case of flagrant and serious violation of the law in force. No one shall be deported except in accordance with the law;

(j) The right to a fair and equitable trial, the right for petition to the Emporer and the right of appeal to the Emporer for commutation of death sentences;

(k) Retroactivity of penal law shall be excluded;

The respect for the rights and freedoms of others and the

requirements of public order and the general welfare alone will justify any limitations to the above rights.

8. Paragraphs 1 to 7 inclusive of the present resolution shall constitute the Federal Act which shall be submitted to the Emporer of Ethiopia for ratification.

APPENDIX 2

Documents of the EPLF

● **Appendix 2a: The National Democratic Programme of the EPLF, 31 January 1977.**

OBJECTIVES

1. ESTABLISH A PEOPLE'S DEMOCRATIC STATE

A. Abolish the Ethiopian colonial administrative organs and all anti-national and undemocratic laws as well as nullify the military, economic and political treaties affecting Eritrea signed between colonial Ethiopia and other governments.

B. Safeguard the interests of the masses of workers, peasants and other democratic forces.

C. Set up a People's Assembly constituted of people's representatives democratically and freely elected from anti-feudal and anti-imperialist patriotic forces. The People's Assembly shall draw up the constitution, promulgate laws, elect the people's administration and ratify national economic plans and new treaties.

D. Protect the people's democratic rights — freedom of speech, the press, assembly, worship and peaceful demonstration; develop anti-feudal and anti-imperialist worker, peasant, women, student and youth organisations.

E. Assure all Eritrean citizens equality before the law without distinction as to nationality, tribe, region, sex, cultural level, occupation, position, wealth, faith, etc.

F. Severely punish Eritrean lackeys of Ethiopian colonialism who have committed crimes against the nation and the people.

2. BUILD AN INDEPENDENT, SELF-RELIANT AND PLANNED NATIONAL ECONOMY

A. Agriculture

1. Confiscate all land in the hands of the aggressor Ethiopian regime, the imperialists, zionists and Eritrean lackeys and put it in the service of the Eritrean masses.

2. Make big nationalised farms and extensive farms requiring modern techniques state-farms and use their produce for the benefit of the masses.

3. Abolish feudal land relations and carry out an equitable

distribution of land. Strive to introduce cooperative farms by creating conditions of cooperation and mutual assistance so as to develop a modern and advanced system of agriculture and animal husbandry capable of increasing the income and improving the lot of the peasantry.

4. Induce the peasants to adopt modern agricultural techniques, introduce them to advanced agricultural implements and provide them with advisors, experts, veterinary services, fertilizers, wells, dams, transportation, finance, etc., in order to alleviate their problems and improve their livelihood and working conditions.

5. Provide the nomads with veterinary services, livestock breeding experts, agricultural advisors and financial assistance in order to enable them to lead settled lives, adopt modern techniques of agriculture and animal husbandry and improve their livelihood.

6. Provide for the peaceful and amicable settlement of land disputes and inequality among individuals and villages in such a way as to harmonize the interest of the aggrieved with that of the national economic interest.

7. Advance the economic and living conditions in, and bridge the gap between, the cities and the countryside.

8. Make pastures and forests state property, preserve wild life and forestry, and fight soil erosion.

9. Maintain a proper balance between agriculture and industry in the context of the planned economy.

10. Promote an association that will organise, politicise and arm the peasants with a clear revolutionary outlook so they can fully participate in the anti-colonial and anti-feudal struggle, defend the gains of the revolution, free themselves from oppression and economic exploitation, and manage their own affairs.

B. Industry

1. Nationalise all industries in the hands of the imperialists, zionists, Ethiopian colonialists and their Eritrean lackeys as well as resident aliens opposed to Eritrean independence.

2. Nationalise big industries, ports, mines, public transport, communications, power plants and other basic economic resources.

3. Exploit marine resources, expand the production of salt and other minerals, develop the fish industry, explore oil and other minerals.

4. Allow nationals who were not opposed to the independence of Eritrea to participate in national construction by owning small factories and workshops compatible with national development and the system of administration.

5. Strive to develop heavy industry so as to promote light industry, advance agriculture and combat industrial dependence.

C. Finance

1. Nationalise all insurance companies and banks, so as to centralise banking operations, regulate economic activities and accelerate economic development.

2. Establish a government-owned central national bank and issue an independent national currency.

3. Prohibit usury in all forms and extend credit at the lowest interest in order to eliminate the attendant exploitation of the masses.

4. Design and implement an appropriate tariffs policy to secure the domestic market for the nation's agricultural, industrial and handicraft products.

5. Formulate and implement an equitable and rational taxation policy to administer and defend the country, carry out production and social functions.

D. Trade

1. Construct essential land, air and sea transportation and communications to develop the nation's trade.

2. Handle all import and export trade.

3. Nationalise the big trading companies and regulate the small ones.

4. Prohibit the export of essential commodities and limit the import of luxury goods.

5. Regulate the exchange and pricing of the various domestic products.

6. Strictly prohibit contraband trade.

7. Establish trade relations with all countries that respect Eritrean sovereignty irrespective of political systems.

E. Urban Land and Housing

1. Make urban land state property.

2. Nationalise all excess urban houses in order to abolish exploitation through rent and improve the livelihood of the masses.

3. Set, taking the standard of living into account, a rational rent price in order to improve the living conditions of the masses.

4. Compensate citizens for nationalised property in accordance with a procedure based on personal income and the condition of the national economy.

5. Build appropriate modern houses to alleviate the shortage of housing for the masses.

3. DEVELOP CULTURE, EDUCATION, TECHNOLOGY AND PUBLIC HEALTH

A. Culture

1. Obliterate the decadent culture and disgraceful social habits that

Ethiopian colonialism, world imperialism and zionism have spread in order to subjugate and exploit the Ethiopian people and destroy their identity.

2. In the new educational curriculum, provide for the proper dissemination, respect and development of the history of Eritrea and its people, the struggle against colonialism, oppression and for national independence, the experience, sacrifices and heroism as well as the national folklore, traditions and culture of the Eritrean people.

3. Destroy the bad aspects of the culture and traditions of Eritrean society and develop its good and progressive content.

4. Ensure that the Eritrean people glorify and eternally cherish the memory of heroic martyrs of the struggle for independence who, guided by revolutionary principles, gave their lives for the salvation of their people and country.

B. Education and Technology

1. Combat illiteracy to free the Eritrean people from the darkness of ignorance.

2. Provide for universal compulsory education up to the middle school.

3. Establish institutions of higher education in the various fields of science, arts, technology, agriculture, etc.

4. Grant students scholarships to pursue studies in the various fields of learning.

5. Establish schools in the various regions of Eritrea in accordance with the need.

6. Separate education from religion.

7. Make the state run all the schools and provide free education at all levels.

8. Integrate education with production and put it in the service of the masses.

9. Enable nationals, especially the students and youth, to train and develop themselves in the sciences, literature, handicrafts and technology through the formation of their own organisations.

10. Provide favourable work conditions for experts and the skilled to enable them to utilise their skills and knowledge in the service of the masses.

11. Engage in educational, cultural and technological exchange with other countries on the basis of mutual benefit and equality.

C. Public Health

1. Render medical services freely to the people.

2. Eradicate contagious diseases and promote public health by building the necessary hospitals and health centres all over Eritrea.

3. Scientifically develop traditional medicine.

4. Establish sports and athletic facilities and popularise them among the masses.

4. SAFEGUARD SOCIAL RIGHTS

A. *Workers' Rights*

1. Politicise and organise the workers, whose participation in the struggle had been hindered by the reactionary line and leaderships, and enable them in a higher and more organised form, to play their vanguard role in the revolution.

2. Abolish the system of labour laws and sham trade unions set up by Ethiopian colonialism and its imperialist masters to exploit and oppress Eritrean workers.

3. Enforce an eight-hour working day and protect the right of workers to rest for one day a week and twenty five days a year.

4. Promulgate a special labour code that properly protects the rights of workers and enables them to form unions.

5. Assure workers comfortable housing and decent living conditions.

6. Devise a social security programme to care for and assist workers, who, because of illness, disability or age, are unable to work.

7. Prohibit unjustified dismissals and undue pay cuts.

8. Protect the right of workers to participate in the management and administration of enterprises and industries.

9. Struggle to eliminate unemployment and protect every citizen's right to work.

B. *Women's Rights*

1. Develop an association through which women can participate in the struggle against colonial aggression and for social transformation.

2. Outline a broad programme to free women from domestic confinement, develop their participation in social production, and raise their political, cultural and technical levels.

3. Assure women full rights of equality with men in politics, economy and social life as well as equal pay for equal work.

4. Promulgate progressive marriage and family laws.

5. Protect the right of women workers to two months' maternity leave with full pay.

6. Protect the rights of mothers and children, provide delivery, nursery and kindergarten services.

7. Fight to eradicate prostitution.

8. Respect the right of women not to engage in work harmful to their health.

9. Design programmes to increase the number and upgrade the quality of women leaders and public servants.

C. *Families of Martyrs, Disabled Fighters and Others Needing Social Assistance*

1. Provide necessary care and assistance to all fighters and other citizens who, in the course of the struggle against Ethiopian colonialism and for national salvation, have suffered disability in jails or in armed combat.

2. Provide assistance and relief to the victims of Ethiopian colonial aggression, orphans, the old and the disabled as well as those harmed by natural causes.

3. Render necessary assistance and care for the families of martyrs.

5. ENSURE THE QUALITY AND CONSOLIDATE THE UNITY OF NATIONALITIES

A. Abolish the system and laws instituted by imperialism, Ethiopian colonialism and their lackeys in order to divide, oppress and exploit the Eritrean people.

B. Rectify all errors committed by opportunists in the course of the struggle.

C. Combat national chauvinism as well as narrow nationalism.

D. Nurture and strengthen the unity and fraternity of Eritrean nationalities.

E. Accord all nationalities equal rights and responsibilities in leading them toward national progress and salvation.

F. Train cadres from all nationalities in various fields to assure common progress.

G. Safeguard the right of all nationalities to preserve and develop their spoken or written language.

H. Safeguard the right of all nationalities to preserve and develop their progressive culture and traditions.

I. Forcefully oppose those who, in the pursuit of their own interests, create cliques on the basis of nationality, tribe, region, etc, and obstruct the unity of the revolution and the people.

6. BUILD A STRONG PEOPLE'S ARMY

A. Liberate the land and the people step by step through the strategy of people's war. Build a strong land, air and naval force capable of defending the country's borders, territorial waters, air space and territorial integrity as well as the full independence, progress and dignity of its people in order to attain prosperity and reach the highest economic stage. The people's army shall be:

- politically conscious, imbued with comradely relations, steeled through revolutionary discipline,

- full of resoluteness, imbued with a spirit of self-sacrifice, participating in production, and

- equipped with modern tactics, weapons and skills.Being the defender of the interests of the workers and peasants, it serves the entire people of Eritrea irrespective of religion, nationality or sex. The basis of this army is the revolutionary force presently fighting for national independence and liberation.

B. Establish a people's militia to safeguard the gains of the revolution and support the People's Army in the liberated and semi-liberated areas.

C. Establish a progressive and advanced military academy.

7. RESPECT FREEDOM OF RELIGION AND FAITH

A. Safeguard every citizen's freedom of religion and belief.

B. Completely separate religion from the state and politics.

C. Separate religion from education and allow no compulsory religious education.

D. Strictly oppose all the imperialist-created new counter-revolutionary faiths, such as Jehovas' Witness, Pentecostal, Bahai, etc.

E. Legally punish those who try to sow discord in the struggle and undermine the progress of the Eritrean people on the basis of religion whether in the course of the armed struggle or in a people's democratic Eritrea.

8. PROVIDE HUMANE TREATMENT TO PRISONERS OF WAR AND ENCOURAGE THE DESERTION OF ERITREAN SOLDIERS SERVING THE ENEMY

A. Oppose the efforts of Ethiopian colonialism to conscript duped soldiers to serve as tools of aggression for the oppression and slaughter of the Eritrean people.

B. Encourage Eritrean soldiers and plainclothesmen who have been duped into serving in the Ethiopian colonial army to return to the just cause and join their people in the struggle against Ethiopian aggression and welcome them to its ranks with full right of equality.

C. Provide humane treatment and care for Ethiopian war prisoners.

D. Severely punish the die-hard, criminal and atrocious henchmen and lackeys of Ethiopian colonialism.

9. PROTECT THE RIGHTS OF ERITREANS RESIDING ABROAD

A. Struggle to organise Eritreans residing abroad in the already formed mass organisations so they can participate in the patriotic anti-colonial struggle

B. Strive to secure the rights of Eritrean refugees in the neighbouring countries, win them the assistance of international organisations, and work for the improvement of their living conditions.

C. Welcome nationals who want to return to their country and participate in their people's daily struggles and advances.

D. Encourage the return and create the means for the rehabilitation of Eritreans forced to flee their country and land by the vicious aggression and oppression of Ethiopian colonialism.

10. RESPECT THE RIGHTS OF FOREIGNERS RESIDING IN ERITREA

A. Grant full rights of residence and work to aliens who have openly or covertly supported the Eritrean people's struggle against Ethiopian colonial oppression and for national salvation and are willing to live in harmony with the legal system to be established.

B. Mercilessly punish aliens who, as lackeys and followers of Ethiopian colonialism, imperialism and zionism, spy on or become obstacles to the Eritrean people.

11. PURSUE A FOREIGN POLICY OF PEACE AND NON-ALIGNMENT

A. Welcome the assistance of any country or organisation which recognises and supports the just struggle of the Eritrean people without interference in its internal affairs.

B. Establish diplomatic relations with all countries irrespective of political and economic system on the basis of the following five principles:
- Respect for each other's independence, territorial integrity, and national sovereignty;
- Mutual non-aggression;
- Non-interference in internal affairs;
- Equality and mutual benefit;
- Peaceful co-existence.

C. Establish good friendly relations with all neighbours.

D. Expand cultural, economic and technological ties with all countries of the world compatible with national sovereignty and independence based on equality. Do not align with any world military bloc or allow the establishment of any foreign military bases on Eritrean soil.

E. Support all just and revolutionary movements, as our struggle is an integral part of the international revolutionary movement in general, and the struggle of the African, Asian and Latin American peoples against colonialism, imperialism, zionism and racial discrimination in particular.

VICTORY TO THE MASSES!
Adopted by the First Congress of the EPLF on January 31st, 1977

● Appendix 2b: The EPLF Unity Proposal, 22 October 1980.

POLITICAL

The Eritrean People's Liberation Front proposes:

1. — Realizing that the unity of the Eritrean people is a fundamental condition for victory, prosperity, peace and progress both in the on-going stage of national democratic revolution where the Eritrean people are conducting armed struggle as well as later;
Rejecting all lines that employ unpatriotic and divisive narrow tendencies, their protagonists, and the machinations and pressures of external forces made in collusion to reinforce fragmentation;A coalition be formed of all the forces and patriotic elements that abide by the above-stated two principles;
2. — The coalition shall form one Eritrean National Assembly composed of representatives of its constituent forces;
3. — The National Assembly shall formulate a political line that would oppose all attempts and ploys aimed at dividing the Eritrean people and mobilize them against their enemies; prepare the conducive platform for different political organizations to propagate their convictions and conduct democratic struggle in the national interest; and ratify the democratic order and institutional components of independent Eritrea;
4. — The National Assembly shall form — a permanent or periodically elected — body that would represent the Eritrean people in all international fora and work to solicit, on behalf of the Eritrean revolution, diplomatic, political, material and humanitarian assistance.
The EPLF expresses its readiness for bilateral meetings with the concerned forces towards the concretization of this proposal and for the elaboration of its details.
MILITARY
- Since the formation of one army and military strategy in order to defeat the colonial regime and achieve liberation is a central theme of the armed struggle of the Eritrean people;
- As this has been demonstrated by the constructive efforts undertaken to reduce schisms and form one organization and, through this, establish one army and formulate one strategy on the

one hand, and the enormous losses incurred in the incessant clashes and bloodletting by the internal and external forces with a vested interest in further fragmentation on the other hand;

- Moreover, in the future too, and the existence of various armies — whether big or small — would have no positive result other than breeding internecine strife and the consequent weakening of the human and material military capabilities of the Eritrean people in the interests of their enemies;

- And permanently, since it would constitute the main obstacle to national political and economic security and stability;

- The EPLF calls upon all those armed forces outside the EPLA who adhere to the above-stated principles and accept their undeniable historical truth to join ranks in the trenches of the Eritrean People's Liberation Army. Their political question having been solved on the basis of the provisions stipulated in the political section of this proposal, the views they might harbour on the military liberation strategy would be accepted subsequent to discussions.

The EPLF invites — through this proposal — to the platform of dialogue all the forces who, aware of the complex phase the Eritrean revolution is currently undergoing, are ready to shed narrow and sectarian interests and pay the necessary sacrifices for the just national rights of the Eritrean people. It reminds all the forces who, defying these objectives, divide the Eritrean people through various ploys, have opted to barter the Eritrean cause as a means of life and belligerently unsheath their sword against the EPLF, to reconsider their positions. The EPLF calls upon all the forces who have given their genuine support to the just cause of the Eritrean people to support this proposal and play an active and constructive role in its implementation.

Political Bureau of the EPLF 25/10/1982.

● Appendix 2c: The EPLF Referendum Proposal, 22 November 1980.

Although the Eritrean revolution has repeatedly reaffirmed its genuine readiness to find a peaceful political solution for the Eritrean question, the Ethiopian regime's unwillingness to seek a peaceful solution and its strivings to crush the Eritrean revolution through active military force and diplomatic conspiracy have doomed all endeavours to failure. Besides, at times when several governments, supporting the correct, democratic and just principle of the right to self-determination, attempted to bring about a genuine peaceful solution, others have created obstacles by trying to impose incorrect and unjust solutions. Thus, there has been no successful or fruitful initiative as yet. For this reason, the killing and suffering of the Eritrean people have not ceased and no stability and peace secured.

Having recognised and assessed these facts, the Eritrean People's Liberation Front (EPLF) would like to present the following important proposal.

First, to bring about a peaceful political solution for the Eritrean question, hold a referendum in Eritrea in accordance with the just, democratic and correct principle of the right of peoples to self-determination;

Second, to implement the first point, set up an international commission acceptable to the Ethiopian government and the Eritrean revolution. Its composition would be subject to discussion and could be formed from the UN, the OAU, the Arab League or the Non-Aligned Movement;

Third, reach agreement on a ceasefire and declare it before holding the referendum, and the commission to be set up in accordance with the second point shall monitor and oversee the ceasefire;

Fourth, from the moment the ceasefire is declared upto the time the referendum is completed, both the Ethiopian regime and the Eritrean revolution should have the freedom to carry out political agitation in all zones where there are Eritreans, with all acts of forcible imposition of views prohibited for both sides so the people may express their views with complete freedom;

Fifth, the time, places, procedure of registration and method of voting, to be determined and formulated by the commission, are to be announced;

Sixth, voting should be based on the following three points:
1. For full independence,
2. For federal association with Ethiopia,
3. For regional autonomy;

Seventh, for any outcome, the Eritrean people should freely elect their representatives and establish an independent state or administration through a constituent assembly.

That this proposal embodies the shortest, best and most reliable road to the peaceful political resolution of the Eritrean question is beyond doubt. Through this declaration, the EPLF calls upon all forces who wish to achieve a peaceful solution for the Eritrean question, support the right to self-determination, and fight for democracy and justice, to contribute their unswerving effort to translate this proposal into action.

● **Appendix 2d: Sixth Regular Session of the Central Committee of the EPLF, 8-11 September 1984 (Excerpts only).**

ON THE GLOBAL LEVEL:
● Aware of the weight and influence of the US and the Soviet Union on a global scale;
● Recalling that the US had masterminded the 'federal'

association of Eritrea with the expansionist and client regime of Haile Selassie in 1952 against the wishes of the Eritrean people and later encouraged that regime to abrogate the 'federation', which had no recourse but the UN, and reduce Eritrea into a colony;

● Noting the economic assistance and diplomatic and propaganda cover that the US, even after the downfall of the Haile Selassie regime, extends the present Ethiopian military regime under the policy of 'detaching it from the Soviet Union and winning it over';

● Noting the injustices that the Soviet Union, oblivious of its just historic stand in 1950 supporting independence for Eritrea, is today committing against the Eritrean people and their revolution for the sake of its global strategy by providing the Derg's colonial regime with weapons of mass destruction to suppress the legitimate, just and human rights of the Eritrean people;

● Recalling further that the intervention of the US and the Soviet Union in the Horn of Africa has created continuous instability, denied peace to the peoples of the region and made them victims of destruction, suffering and emigration:

The Central Committee calls on the US and the Soviet Union to:

● Recognize the Eritrean people's legitimate, just and human right to self-determination;

● Halt the political, military and economic assistance as well as diplomatic and propaganda cover with which they are providing the Ethiopian colonial regime in order to suppress the right of the Eritrean people and crush their struggle;

● Support the endeavours to resolve the Eritrean question by a just and peaceful means;

● Stop their intervention in the Horn of Africa, with all its consequences of death, destruction and complications, and support the efforts to bring peace and stability that secures the interests of the peoples of the region.

ON THE EPLF:

As the decisive force of the Eritrean revolution and the genuine representative of the aspirations of the Eritrean people, affirms its determination to:

● Strictly adhere to its policy of non-alignment to ensure that the Eritrean revolution shall never be an instrument of foreign interests.

ON THE UN:

● Demands that the UN, as the primary world body legally answerable for the Eritrean question, shoulder the responsibility that it has so far evaded and table the just case of the Eritrean people in its agenda with a view to resolving it.

ON EUROPE:

● Appreciating the political, material and humanitarian assistance that states, political parties and other organizations in Europe have extended to the Eritrean people's struggle;

● Hailing the resolution of the European Parliament which supports the Eritrean people's just cause for self-determination, condemns the Derg's military offensives and calls for a peaceful solution of the Eritrean question; and

● Reminding certain governments which, through their support for the Derg's regime and their intervention, perpetrate injustices against the Eritrean people's just struggle and cause further instability in the Horn of Africa to reconsider their position;Calls upon the European states, political parties and other organizations to:

● Support the just struggle of the Eritrean people;

● Condemn the continuous military offensives of the Ethiopian regime;

● Support the efforts for a just peaceful solution for the Eritrean people's cause;

● Extend and increase their material and humanitarian assistance to the Eritrean people;

● Oppose the prevailing global and regional intervention that has become the cause of instability, destruction and emigration; and

● Play a positive role in the endeavours to bring about peace and stability for the interests of the peoples of the Horn of Africa.

ON THE NATIONAL AND MULTI-NATIONAL MOVEMENTS IN ETHIOPIA:

● Convinced that the relationship between the struggles of the Eritrean and Ethiopian peoples is based on solidarity for liberation and democracy;

● Affirming that it does not view the solidarity of struggle of the Eritrean and Ethiopian peoples through the narrow prism of temporary convenience of give and take;

● Reaffirming that its conviction of this solidarity does not waver on account of any external influences and narrow temporary advantages; and

● Reaffirming further that it supports the democratic solidarity obtaining between the national and multi-national Ethiopian movements so as to lead to the voluntary establishment and building of a democratic regime based on equality;

Urges all the national and multi-national movements to:

● Base their mutual relations on clear long-range perspectives and a firm ground free from the tactics of mutual utilization; and

● While affirming its determination to actively struggle to further consolidate and upgrade the solidarity, it calls on them to strengthen their solidarity with the Eritrean people's struggle and its leading organization, the EPLF.

A JUST PEACEFUL SOLUTION FOR THE ERITREAN QUESTION:

- Recalling that the Eritrean people are peace and justice loving and that they rose up in arms only when their perseverant political struggles were suppressed through backward and barbarous repression;
- Recalling that peace has, side by side with the armed struggle, been their constant call and noting that they have, from time to time, paid positive attention to the question of peace;
- Recalling the efforts made in Berlin with the mediation of third parties;
- Recalling the attempts of third parties even after Berlin, orchestrated under the guise of peace but intended to aggravate the internal divisions of the Eritrean revolution; and
- Noting that it has subsequently been playing an active role by engaging in preliminary contacts to create an atmosphere conducive to negotiations;

Reaffirms its readiness to engage in relentless endeavours and continuous contacts to create a favourable groundwork for reaching a just peaceful solution on the basis of the principle of the right of peoples to self-determination as well as its correct proposal of 21.11.80 for an internationally supervised referendum.

Calls on all concerned as well as peace and justice loving forces to play an active role in support of its struggles for a just peace.

The Central Committee
EPLF
11.09.1984

APPENDIX 3

Documents of the Ethiopian Government

● **Appendix 3a: The Programme of the Ethiopian National Democratic Revolution, April 1976. (Paragraph 5 — on the nationalities)**

The right to self-determination of all nationalities will be recognized and fully respected. No nationality will dominate another one since the history, culture, language and religion of each nationality will have equal recognition in accordance with the spirit of socialism. The unity of Ethiopia's nationalities will be based on their common struggle against feudalism, imperialism, bureaucratic capitalism and all reactionary forces. This united struggle is based on the desire to construct a new life and a new society based on equality, brotherhood and mutual respect.

Nationalities on border areas and those scattered over various regions have been subjected to special subjugation for a long time. Special attention will be made to raise the political, economic and cultural life of these nationalities. All necessary steps to equalize these nationalities with the other nationalities of Ethiopia will be undertaken.

Given Ethiopia's existing situation, the problem of nationalities can be resolved if each nationality is accorded full right to self-government. This means that each nationality will have regional autonomy to decide on matters concerning its internal affairs. Within its environs, it has the right to determine the contents of its political, economic and social life, use its own language and elect its own leaders and administrators to head its internal organs.

The right of self-government of nationalities will be implemented in accordance with all democratic procedures and principles.

● **Appendix 3b: The Ethiopian 'Nine Point Peace Place' of 18 May 1976.**

Policy declaration of the Provisional Military Government to solve the problem in the administrative region of Eritrea in a peaceful way.

It is an indelible historical fact that the northern region of Ethiopia, called Eritrea for the last 87 years, had been the seat of the history, culture and administration of ancient Ethiopia. However, because of its location along the Red Sea and the strategic importance of its sea coast, the northern region of Ethiopia had been coveted by various forces during the last few centuries...

During the federation, the despotic government of Haile Selassie extended its oppressive rule to Eritrea. The peoples of the region who had fought 'to get rid of colonial rule and live in freedom with the motherland', were stripped of their democratic rights, and step by step were put under the yoke of feudalism and imperialism. This created a favourable situation for those forces opposed to the unity of the Ethiopian people. It was obvious that, as the oppression continued to increase, internal contradictions served as a means for external enemies to sneak in; a movement for separation that was started by the colonial rulers continued to grow with the help of foreign governments who had expansionist interest and envied Eritrea for its strategic importance.

From the very beginning the secessionist movement included reactionary leaders who were instruments of colonial rulers and expansionist forces interested in the strategic importance of Eritrea. As the movement grew in age, progressive groups are known to have joined it as the result of the opposition to the economic, social and political oppression perpetrated against the broad masses by feudalism and imperialism.

It is also true that there are reactionary and progressive groups within the movement with irreconcilable views on political questions, external relations and matters pertaining to contradictions among the people in Eritrea region. It is an undeniable truth that the reactionary group which, for its own benefit and comfort, has become servile to the strategic interest of expansionist forces has been exploiting religious differences and contradictions among nationalities. This group had caused the loss of lives of numerous innocent Eritreans every time it launched an attack against the progressive group...

In accordance with the Programme of the Ethiopian National Democratic Revolution and the repeated revolutionary calls in the past, the Provisional Military Government has made the following decisions to provide a peaceful solution to the problem in the Administrative Region of Eritrea:

Decision

1. The anomalies which had existed before will be done away with and the people of the Eritrean Administrative Region will, in a new spirit and in co-operation and collaboration with the rest of the Ethiopian people, have full participation in the political, economic and social life of the country. They will in particular play their full role in the struggle to establish the People's Democratic Republic

in accordance with the Programme of the Ethiopian Democratic Revolution.

2. The Programme of the Ethiopian National Democratic Revolution has affirmed that the right of self-determination of nationalities can be guaranteed through regional autonomy which takes due account of objective realities prevailing in Ethiopia, her surroundings and in the world at large. To translate this into deeds, the Government will study each of the regions of the country, the history and interactions of the nationalities inhabiting them, their geographic positions, economic structures and their suitability for development and administration. After taking these into consideration, the Government will at an appropriate time present to the people the structure of the regions that can exist in the future. The entire Ethiopian people will then democratically discuss the issue at various levels and decide upon it themselves.

3. Having realised the difficulties existing in the Administrative Region of Eritrea and the urgency of overcoming them, and in order to apply in practice the right of self-determination of nationalities on a priority basis, the Provisional Military Government is prepared to discuss and exchange views with the progressive groups and organizations in Eritrea which are not in collusion with feudalists, reactionary forces in the neighbourhood and imperialists.

4. The Government will give full support to progressives in the Eritrean Administrative Region who will, in collaboration with the progressives in the rest of Ethiopia and on the basis of the programme of the Ethiopian National Democratic Revolution, endeavour to arouse, organise and lead the working masses of the region in the struggle against the three enemies of the Ethiopian people — feudalism, bureaucratic capitalism and imperialism — and thereby promote the unity of the oppressed classes of Ethiopia.

5. The Government will give all necessary assistance to those Ethiopians who, because of the absence of peace in the Eritrean Administrative Region for a long time, have been in exile in neighbouring countries and in far-off alien lands so that they may, as of today, return to their own country.

6. The Government will make a special effort in rehabilitating those Ethiopians who might have lost their property because of the adverse conditions that had existed. All those who have been dislocated from jobs and education as a result of the existing problem will be enabled to avail themselves of the employment and educational opportunities which Ethiopia can offer in any part of the country.

7. People who have been imprisoned as a result of the existing problem will be released. The cases of those who have been sentenced to life imprisonment or death will be carefully examined and reviewed as soon as peaceful conditions are restored and, on the basis of their

offences, they will either receive reduced prison terms or be altogether released.

8. The state of emergency will be lifted as soon as the major decisions begin to be implemented and peace is guaranteed in the Eritrean Administrative Region.

9. A special commission entrusted with the task of ensuring the implementation of decisions 5 to 7 above will be established by proclamation.

APPENDIX 4

Conclusions of the Permanent People's Tribunal

Conclusions of the Permanent People's Tribunal Advisory Opinion on Eritrea, 3 Oct 1980 (President: Francois Rigaux; Vice President: Ruth First).

The Tribunal decides:

I. ON THE QUALITY OF BEING A PEOPLE
1. The Eritrean people do not constitute a national minority within a State. They have the characteristics of a people according to the law of the United Nations and the Universal Declaration on the Rights of Peoples.
2. In their quality as a people they have the right to live freely, and without prejudice to its national identity and culture, within the boundaries of their own territory as delimited during the colonial period up to 1950.
3. The identity of the Eritrean people, determined, in particular, by its resistance to Italian colonialism, was recognized by Resolution 390 (V) of the General Assembly of the United Nations.
4. The unity of the Eritrean people is today confirmed by the armed struggle which it has been waging since September 1961, and which has resulted in the liberation of numerous regions of the country, now administered by the national liberation fronts and also in the creation of new economic and social relations.

II. ON THE RIGHT TO SELF-DETERMINATION
5. The Eritrean people are endowed with the inviolable and inalienable right to self-determination.
6. The alleged ancient historical ties between Eritrea and Ethiopia, claimed by the Ethiopian Government are not adequately documented, and are not, at any rate, of such a nature as to constitute an obstacle to the recognition and the exercise of this right to self-determination.
7. The right to self-determination must be exercised without prejudice to the territorial integrity of Eritrea, according to Articles 2 and 3 of the Charter of the Organization of African Unity, and without prejudice to the integrity of the frontiers inherited from colonialism, in accordance with the principles affirmed by the OAU resolution of July 21, 1964.
8. The Federal system, organized in 1950 between Ethiopia and

Eritrea by Resolution 390 (V) of the General Assembly of the United Nations, though recognizing the existence of the Eritrean people and its right to self-determination allowed the strategic and geopolitical interests of some great powers to prevail over this right.

9. From the outset the Ethiopian Government did not respect the provisions of Resolution 390 (V), above all prohibiting the use of national languages and depriving Eritreans of their civil and political rights. The transgression of the Resolution reached its culmination with the unilateral abolition, by the Ethiopian Government, of the federal regime, which brought the Eritrean people under foreign domination, as defined by the law of the United Nations and the Universal Declaration of the Rights of Peoples.

10.The right of the Eritrean people to self-determination does not therefore constitute a form of secession, and can today only be exercised by achieving independence; the will of the Eritrean people having been clearly demonstrated in this regard by the armed struggle which has been carried on by the liberation fronts for nearly 20 years.

III.ON THE DUTIES OF THE INTERNATIONAL COMMUNITY

11.The Eritrean question lies within the competence of the United Nations on two counts: the maintenance of international peace and security, and the obligation to guarantee the respect of the right of peoples to self-determination.

12.The Organization of African Unity has the duty to unreservedly dedicate itself to the cause of the total emancipation of African territories not yet independent, because according to the preamble to the Addis Ababa Charter, all peoples have 'the inalienable right to determine their own destiny'.

13.The Eritrean people's struggle for national liberation is an armed conflict to which apply the general principles of the law of war as resulting from the Geneva Conventions of 1949 and the First Additional Protocol of 1977.

14. By virtue of Article 1 paragraph 2 of the Charter of the United Nations, Resolution 2625 (XXV) and Resolution 3314 (XXIX) of the General Assembly, as well as article 30 of the Universal Declaration on the Rights of the Peoples, the right of the Eritrean people to self-determination imposes on all States and International organisations a double obligation:

- to abstain from all cooperation, military or other, intended to suppress a movement of national liberation;

- to consider it their duty to contribute to self-determination by providing, to that end, every form of diplomatic and material support.

APPENDIX 5

Documents of the European Community

● **Appendix 5a: Excerpts from the report of the Political Affairs Committee of the European Parliament on the Horn of Africa (Rapporteur: Mr C. Ripa di Mena, Italian Socialist Party) 14 December 1983.**

...The Ethiopia-Eritrea conflict originated in the violation by Addis Ababa of a United Nations resolution concerning the arrangements for the decolonization of Eritrea. The violation occurred in 1962. The resolution dates back to 1950. The result has been a cruel and bloody conflict which raises problems of principle in which the whole of Africa feels involved. Europe has a clear duty to support the demands for implementation of the decisions which were adopted in an international forum (and which were also accepted by Ethiopia). Moreover, in view of the immense loss of life, the devastation and the uninterrupted flow of refugees into countries which themselves suffer from extreme poverty, Europe must continue to hope for a cessation of hostilities and for the opening of constructive negotiations able to satisfy the demands of Eritrea without, however, ignoring those of Ethiopia - which is concerned lest a settlement trigger a process of disintegration of the State — and of the African continent as a whole, which is loath to endorse territorial changes imposed by force.

It is perhaps not unrealistic to hope that a settlement of the conflict which avoided humiliating Ethiopia and ensured the peaceful co-existence of the peoples and nations concerned would create conditions that would induce the Soviets and Cubans to leave the area. The end of the conflict might also weaken the role of the military in Addis Ababa, which in turn might facilitate the start of a process of internal democratization or, at least, the emergence of a regime which is more open and more willing to respect human rights...

The problem of Eritrea

The decolonisation of Eritrea — 120,000 km² and a population of about 3.5 million — was hotly contested. The four main victorious powers of the Second World War failed to reach agreement on its future, even though the former colonial power, Italy, had surrendered all claims to the territory, as also to its other former colonies, with the signing of the peace treaty. It was not until 1950 that an agreement was reached in the United Nations, which was, however, adopted only after an extremely controversial debate. The essence of this agreement was that Eritrea should form part of a federal union with Ethiopia, under the Ethiopian Crown. The Federation came into being in 1952 and existed, despite various vicissitudes, for a decade. In 1962, following military intervention by Ethiopia, the Eritrean parliament was dissolved. The Federation then ceased to exist and Eritrea lost its autonomy, becoming a mere province of the empire.

From the point of view of international law, the Ethiopian action was totally illegal, since it violated an unequivocal resolution of the United Nations. It also violated the principle, which is one of the most solid bases of relations between the African countries, of the inviolability of the colonial frontiers, bearing in mind that at the time of the final decision the identity of Eritrea was separate from that of Ethiopia. What is bitterly contested is the specious nationalistic justification of Ethiopia's action, since there are undeniable historical and cultural differences between the Eritrean and Ethiopian peoples (identifiable with the different ethnic groups which had somehow been brought together under the controlling influence of the Ethiopian empire over many centuries). The action was also politically unacceptable, inasmuch as it resulted in internal repression and regional destabilisation.

The annexation of Eritrea provoked the formation of an armed resistance movement. This was initially organized by the Eritrean Liberation Front (ELF). The movement gathered strength over the years, receiving the full support of the population. At the same time, however, political divisions emerged, which subsequently resulted in the creation of countless splinter groups. The ELF has ceased to be the dominant political and military group. The group which has most successfully extended its influence over the territory and population is the Eritrean People's Liberation Front.

Then there are the people's liberation movements, as well as other small groupings. Broadly speaking the ELF derives its inspiration from Islam, while the EPLF is of Marxist persuasion. The ultimate aim of all these groups is independence for Eritrea. They have repeatedly striven to settle their differences (which hinge on the social order to be established by Eritrea once it has won independence). But, although there have been formal declarations of reconciliation, the disagreements have persisted. There have been frequent bloody skirmishes between the different guerrilla movements, particularly in recent times. It is perhaps because of these conflicts that the Eritrean liberation fronts have never attempted to set up a government in exile or in the 'liberated' territories.

Although there are no formal contacts between them, the Eritrean guerrilla movements and Somalia found that they had enough in common to launch, in 1977, a joint offensive against the Addis Ababa central government. This offensive was repulsed after little more than a year's fighting. The Eritrean objectives are, however, very different from the objectives of the Somalis. The former, unlike the latter, are clearly justified from the point of view of international law. Nevertheless, Eritrea's demand for independence gives rise to contradictions, since Ethiopia has invoked the UN's mandatory 'federal' decision and, on the basis of that decision, insists that the problem should be considered as a strictly internal one. Moreover, since fully twenty years have elapsed since the annexation of Eritrea, the principle of the inviolability of frontiers might easily be reinterpreted to strengthen the arguments of those who favour maintaining the status quo. The arguments of the Eritreans, it should be added, carry more credence with the Arab states than with the OAU from which, indeed, they have never evoked much sympathy.

As far as the military operations are concerned, these are not achieving the results which Addis Ababa had hoped: the 'red star' operation, launched in 1982, has more or less failed, while in February 1983 the Tigrean revolt gathered considerable momentum.

Notwithstanding the presence and the military aid of the Eastern bloc countries, it is apparently extremely difficult for the Ethiopians to win an outright military victory. The Eritrean terrain is unsuited to tank offensives and is more favourable to guerrilla warfare operations such as those carried out in Afghanistan. The Ethiopian troops have used Soviet MI-24 helicopters and have been accused by the Eritrean People's Liberation Front of having used toxic gases. These accusations have been denied by the Addis Ababa government and Western observers in the Ethiopian capital have not been able to establish the truth of the matter.

It seems, moreover, that the Soviet Union is reluctant to become deeply involved in the Eritrean problem. Indeed, the 'red star' operation was not approved by the Soviets and observers have pointed out that if Addis Ababa were to succeed in settling once and for all the Eritrean problem by force of arms, it would strengthen the position of the nationalist factions in the Derg and in the army, which for the most part has been antipathetic to the Soviet presence.

Aside from the military measures, there is an economic objective in Menghistu's strategy, which is to 'rebuild Eritrea', the aim being to weaken the resolve of the rebels by offering an alternative course to the Eritrean people which would involve improving their standard of living etc. The achievement of such an objective would be plainly difficult, both because of the enormous destruction caused by the war and because the prevailing situation is a disincentive to investment.

The Eritrean liberation movements receive very little aid from other countries. The United States is unwilling to get caught up in the conflict, apparently for two reasons. Firstly, it is likely that Israel would be hostile to US intervention, since it would not like to see the establishment of another Arab state in the area of the straits leading into the Red Sea. Secondly, the USA is convinced that, since the Soviet system is unpalatable to Africa as whole, the end of the Eritrean revolt would induce the Soviets to withdraw from Ethiopia, just as they have already been forced to withdraw from Egypt, the Sudan and Somalia.

In these circumstances, the Eritreans have obtained what little support they have from certain Arab states, which are nevertheless antagonistic to the principle so firmly defended by the Organization of African Unity (OAU), that of the inviolability of the frontiers established at the end of the colonial period.

Nevertheless, the Sudan has played a major part in the conflict by allowing the Eritrean liberation forces to take refuge on Sudanese territory. Although there have been attempts to reconcile the interests of Ethiopia and the Sudan, the results have been disappointing and the situation between the two countries today is one of stalemate. The Sudan has recently accused Ethiopia of supporting the rebel forces in the south.

In sum, the war in Eritrea is a source of tensions and severe economic and social problems, not just because there is still no prospect of an end to the conflict, but also because it has created an enormous refugee problem. There are at least 500,000 refugees, most of whom have been taken in by the Sudan...

CONCLUSIONS

As has been shown in the foregoing pages, the problems of the Horn of Africa will be extremely difficult to solve. Yet, despite their exceptional complexity, the European Community cannot remain indifferent to them. While for the Ten there are strategic interests at stake, it cannot be forgotten that the countries of the region — Ethiopia, Somalia and Djibouti, but also the Sudan and Kenya — are signatories to the Convention of Lome and as such closely associated with the Community.

The Ten must firmly condemn the countless interventions of the Eastern bloc countries, which have triggered in the region a process of major power confrontation and rearmament.

The Ten should bring pressure to bear on the Soviet Union in the hope of persuading it to withdraw its own troops and those of its allies and to help the international community resolve the tragic and destabilizing refugee problem.

By virtue of their former colonial interests, some of the Community Member States still maintain more or less close relations with the countries of the Horn of Africa. Yet a common position allowing a concerted response and concerted action on the part of the Ten would still seem to be lacking. Consequently, the first step should be to introduce a common programme of action to promote a settlement of the prevailing conflicts, particularly that between Ethiopia and Eritrea. Since, however, the situation is so complex and so delicate, it is plain that the Community must proceed with extreme caution and pursue a policy of mediation based on the accepted rules of diplomacy.

The Ten should also exert discreet but firm pressure on the governments of the region with a view to securing respect for human rights, both generally and in specific cases and situations. Special efforts should be made to protect human rights in Ethiopia, since it is in that country that the gravest violations seem to have occurred. One of the most distressing problems of the region, in both moral and human terms, is that of the refugee camps which, by their very nature, also pose a threat to stability; indeed, the existence of these camps could well create a Palestinian-type situation, which would have perilous consequence both for the host countries and for the region as a whole.

● Appendix 5b: Excerpts from Resolution of the European Parliament on the Horn of Africa, 12 April 1984.

The European Parliament
- noting the strategic importance of the Horn of Africa for both Western countries and the Eastern bloc, being adjacent to the Arabian peninsular,
- concerned about the 20-year old conflict between the Ethiopian state and the Eritrean resistance, in which Ethiopia is being supported by many thousands of troops and military advisers from the Soviet Union, the German Democratic Republic, Cuba and South Yemen,
- recalling the resolution adopted by the Assembly of the United Nations on 2 December 1950 which stated that Eritrea should constitute an autonomous unit federated with Ethiopia and having wide powers over its own internal affairs,
- concerned about the danger of a fragmentation of the Ethiopian State which might render the region of the Horn of Africa and surrounding areas even more unstable,
- alarmed by the growing large-scale militarization of the region of the Horn of Africa, aggravated by Ethiopian policies and military action,
- recalling the resolution of the foreign ministers at the Islamic

Conference in Islamabad in 1980, which called for the withdrawal of Soviet and allied troops from the region and also the removal of foreign bases in the Horn of Africa and the Red Sea and the exclusion of this area from superpower confrontation,
- keenly concerned about the drought and famine afflicting the peoples of Ethiopia, Somalia and Djibouti,
- greatly alarmed by the plight of refugees in the Horn of Africa and neighbouring countries such as the Sudan,
- stressing the fact that Community aid, particularly food aid, contributed largely to ensuring the survival of the peoples of that area, who were the victims of drought and political conflicts simultaneously,
- pointing out that the European Parliament delegation which went to the area in June 1983 noted that aid, particularly food aid, is being properly used in Ethiopia, Djibouti and Somalia,
- concerned about the human rights situation in the region, particularly in Ethiopia,...
1. Strongly condemns the multiple interventions of the Soviet Union and the countries of the Eastern bloc in the Horn of Africa and the stationing and use in action of troops from the Soviet Union, Cuba, The German Democratic Republic and South Yemen,
2. Invites all the great powers not to make this region a place of confrontation and rearmament,
3. Asks the Foreign Ministers meeting in political cooperation and the Council of Ministers as such:
(a) to adopt a common standpoint on the problems of the Horn of Africa in order to take all such initiatives as may contribute to a solution of the conflicts and the re-establishment of friendly relations between the states and ethnic groups of the region,
(b) to bring pressure to bear on the Soviet Union to withdraw its troops and those of countries allied to it from Ethiopia and to work together with the international community to aid the refugees and the people threatened by famine,
(c) to strongly urge the Ethiopian Government to find a peaceful and negotiated solution of the conflict between it and the Eritrean peoples which takes account of their identity, as recognised by the United Nations resolution of 2 December 1950, and is consistent with the basic principles of the OAU,...
4. Calls on the European Community, in consultation with the UNHCR, to take active measures to solve the problems of the refugees in the region as proposed by the delegation of the European Parliament in June 1983;
5. Calls on the Commission to maintain and increase its food aid for the countries of the region, including Sudan, and for the peoples of Eritrea and Tigra, both of them being severely affected not only

by drought and famine, but also by military conflict, and to ensure that the means of its distribution are improved;

6. Invites the European Community to do all in its power to help Ethiopia, Somalia and the United Nations High Commissioner for Refugees to reach a tripartite agreement on the voluntary repatriation of Ethiopian refugees in Somalia;

7. Asks the Commission of the European Communities to take all necessary steps to ensure that the humanitarian aid granted reaches all the people affected, irrespective of their political sympathies;

● **Appendix 5c: Excerpt from the Manifesto of the Confederation of Socialist Parties of the European Community, 9 March 1984.** *European Political Cooperation in Africa.*

The Socialists of the EEC believe that the fundamental interests of all the people concerned, such as the people of Eritrea or the Western Sahara, should be taken into account whilst preparing solutions to regional conflicts.

Documents of the Labour Party

● **Appendix 6a: Labour's Programme 1982.**

Eritrea and Ethiopia

The independent status of the Eritrean people was ended with the revocation of its federal status with Ethiopia in 1962, and since then Eritrea has been run as an integral part of the Ethiopian empire. This was a unilateral act of colonisation which violated the rights of the Eritrean people, who have fiercely fought for their independence. The Eritreans have fought against Ethiopia, which received the backing of the USA and Britain until the overthrow of the empire in 1974. Since that time, it has received financial and military support from the Soviet bloc and Cuba. We support the Eritrean cause for national self-determination. The proposal for an internationally supervised referendum on the future of Eritrea, made by the Eritrean People's Liberation Front, is an acceptable and legitimate means of settling the future of that country. The referendum would allow the Eritrean people to choose between full independence, federal association with Ethiopia and regional autonomy within Ethiopia. We support the struggle for full democratic rights of all the people in Ethiopia.

The next Labour government shall therefore: provide direct financial and material support to the EPLF and the Eritrean Relief Association; work at the United Nations and other international organisations to promote the proposals made by the EPLF for a referendum on the future of Eritrea.

● **Appendix 6b: Statement by the General Secretary of the Labour Party (Ron Hayward) on the occasion of the visit of the EPLF European Representative to London, 23 February 1982.**

Our meeting together here ... is of historic significance. It comes at a tragic and terrible moment in the history of the Eritrean people. Against them the Ethiopians have unleashed an onslaught of unprecedented proportions and ferocity (the sixth offensive)... The Labour National Executive Committee issued the following statement on 9 February.

'The Labour Party is deeply concerned by reports of a sixth offensive being launched by the Ethiopian regime in an attempt to finally crush the Eritrean people's struggle to liberate their homeland. We are particularly alarmed by continuing reports of the imminent use of nerve gas by the Ethiopian forces, and since this has been denied by the Ethiopian authorities, we call for an independent investigation of this question to be conducted by the United Nations as a matter of urgency.'

...The clear anti-colonial position adopted (by the Labour Party in the 1920s) stood the test of time, and it is worth recalling that in the 1930s the Labour Party was in the forefront in denouncing the Italian attack upon, and conquest of, Ethiopia. At the time we condemned the British government for failing to honour our agreements for collective security, and imposed sanctions against Italy.

After the Second World War we played our part in the process of decolonisation. Indeed, many of our most stalwart members, such as Lord Noel Baker and Lord Fenner Brockway, have played leading roles in these campaigns.

We therefore welcomed the emergence of independent Africa, and the formation of the Organisation of African Unity in 1963. We also respect the principle laid down by the OAU that colonial borders, no matter how unsatisfactory, should be accepted and preserved. We understood that if this was not the case, then Africa could be plagued for years to come with conflict and division. But surely it can be argued this principle stands in direct contradiction to our support for Eritrean freedom, since Eritrea is part of Ethiopia.

The key to this apparent contradiction was elaborated by the notable socialist historian — Basil Davidson — when he pointed out that, and I quote:

'Eritrea was not enclosed during the 'colonial partition.' It was enclosed within Ethiopia by the Emporer Haile Selassie in 1962, and its status cannot, therefore, be related to any inheritance of the colonial frontiers.'

In 1962, unilaterally and against United Nations protest, Haile Selassie destroyed Eritrean autonomy reducing the country to an entirely dependent province of his empire.

All local rights and powers were abrogated in favour of direct Amhara rule. This unilateral act of 1962 was, in all respects, one of colonisation within the general meaning of the term.

It is for this reason that we in the Labour Party give our support to the Eritrean cause. As part of the anti-colonial struggle it falls squarely within Labour's long held beliefs.

At the same time it must be recognised that we do not, therefore, turn our backs on Ethiopia. We welcome the Ethiopian revolution, overthrowing a regime that was incapable of meeting the people's needs. Nor should our support for Eritrea be seen as the prelude for a generalised dismantling of the Ethiopian state. The Eritrean struggle is strictly a 'special case' within the whole conflict in the Horn of Africa.

At the same time it must be stated that our relations with Ethiopia will be less than fraternal as long as the Government fails to come to terms with the interests of the different nationalities in Ethiopia. The oppression of these nationalities, as well as the denial of human rights, must inevitably stand in the way of our relations with the Ethiopian revolution.

APPENDIX 7

Resolution of the Socialist International

Resolution from the 16th Congress of the Socialist International, Albufeira, April 7-10 1983 (section on Eritrea and Ethiopia, taken from General Circular No. G4/83E).

Looking at the Horn of Africa, the Socialist International condemns the presence of Soviet, Cuban and East German troops in Ethiopia. The struggle of the Eritrean people for self-determination, which has persisted for 30 years, must be settled by the principles upheld by the United Nations and the OAU.

Glossary

Derg — Amharic word for 'council' and the abbreviation of 'Provisional Military Administrave Council', the ruling body in Ethiopia since 1974.

EDU — Ethiopian Democratic Union, an early opposition group to the Derg led by the feudal chiefs of the Haile Selassie period.

ELF — Eritrean Liberation Front, the only front in Eritrea between 1961 and 1970, now split into numerous small factions, one of which (ELF-CC) cooperates with the EPLF inside Eritrea.

ELF-PLF — Eritrean Liberation Front-Popular Liberation Front, a small group led by Osman Sabbe, with no presence in Eritrea, but able to influence the position of many Arab countries on the conflict.

EPDA — Ethiopian People's Democratic Alliance, a recent opposition group composed of military officers and high ranking government officials of the Haile Selassie period, reported to be sustained by covert US funding.

EPDM - Ethiopian Peoples' Democratic Movement, an offshoot of the EPRP, which in 1984 controls and administers large parts of Wollo and Gondar provinces of Ethiopia.

EPLA - Eritrean People's Liberation Army, the army of the EPLF.

EPLF - Eritrean People's Liberation Front, formed from the groups opposing the ELF leadership, which split from the ELF in 1970, administers 85% of Eritrea in 1984.

EPRP — Ethiopian People's Revolutionary Party, formed an early left-wing opposition to the Derg until crushed by the mass killings and torture carried out on the Derg's orders in 1976-78. The EPRP drew its support from white collar workers, the trade unions and the student population of the towns.

ERA — Eritrean Relief Association, the humanitarian agency which operates in the EPLF-administered areas of Eritrea.

ICRC — International Committee of the Red Cross, based in Geneva.

ME'ISON — Mela Etiopia Socialist Netanake (All-Ethiopia Socialist Movement), initially cooperated with the Derg after the 1974 revolution and was responsible for drafting the Ethiopia National Democratic Programme before being purged in 1977.

OAU — Organisation of African Unity, whose headquarters are in

Addis Ababa.

OLF — Oromo Liberation Front, active in Wollega and Hararghe provinces of Ethiopia.

PDRY — People's Democratic Republic of Yemen.

RRC - Relief and Rehabilitation Commission, the authority in the Ethiopian government with responsibility for relief aid.

TPLF — Tigray People's Liberation Front, the strongest opposition front in Ethiopia, with a large guerrilla army which controls 90% of Tigray province and parts of Gondar and Wollo provinces.

WSLF - Western Somali Liberation Front, still active, in Hararghe and Bale provinces, despite its defeat in the Ogaden War of 1977/78.

Bibliography

A. Books and Articles

AMNESTY INTERNATIONAL, Human Rights Violations in Ethiopia, (Amnesty International, London, 1978).

ARAIA TSEGGAI, Independent Eritrea: Economically Viable, (in Horn of Africa, Vol. VI, No 2).

ASSEFAW TEKESTE, Medicine at War, (in Socialism and Health, Nov/Dec. 1982).

BEREKET HABTE SELASSIE, Conflict and Intervention in the Horn of Africa, (Monthly Review Press, New York and London, 1980).

CATHOLIC INSTITUTE FOR INTERNATIONAL RELATIONS, Comment, Eritrea, (CIIR, London, 1984).

CLIFFE, Lionel and BONDESTAM, Lars, Eritrea: Popular Participation and the Liberation Struggle, (Lelio Basso Foundation, unpublished, 1983).

DAVIDSON, Basil, CLIFFE, Lionel and BEREKET HABTE SELASSIE (Eds.), Behind the War in Eritrea, (Spokesman, Nottingham, 1980).

DINES, Mary, Eritrea, a report on a recent visit, (War on Want, London, 1978).

EISENLOEFFEL, Frits, Famine in Eritrea, (SOH Publications, Utrecht, 1983).

EISENLOEFFEL, Frits, and RONNBACK, Inge, The Eritrean Durrah Odyssey (SOH Publications Utrecht, 1983).

ERITREAN MEDICAL ASSOCIATION, Health Service Delivery in Eritrea, (unpublished, London, 1984).

ERITREAN PEOPLE'S LIBERATION FRONT, Creating a Popular Economic, Political and Military Base, (unpublished, 1982).

---, Department of Social Affairs, (unpublished, 1982).

---, Education under the EPLF, (unpublished, 1982).

---, The Experiences of the EPLF in Pursuing the Policy of Self-Reliance in the Economic Field, (unpublished, 1982).

---, Memorandum, The National Question in Eritrea. (April, 1978).

---, National Democratic Programme, (1977).

---, Towards the Delivery of a Health Service Delivery System in Liberated Eritrea, (EPLF Health Department, 1981).

ERITREA PUBLIC HEALTH PROGRAMME, A Comprehensive Public Health Programme in Rural Eritrea 1982-1985, (unpublished, 1981)

ERITREAN RELIEF ASSOCIATION, Eritrea Drought Report 1983, (ERA, Khartoum, 1984).

EUROPEAN PARLIAMENT, Political Affairs Committee, Report on the Horn of Africa, PE 87.298 (Strasbourg, Oct. 1983).

FENET, Alain, The Right of the Eritrean People to Self-Determination, (CRISPA, Amiens, 1983).

FOUR POWER COMMISSION OF INVESTIGATION FOR THE FORMER ITALIAN COLONIES, Report on Eritrea, (London, 1948).

GILKES, Patrick, The Dying Lion, Feudalism and Modernisation in Ethiopia, (Julian Friedmann Publishers Ltd., London, 1977).

HALCROW WATER (Consulting Engineers), Water Supply Project in Eritrea, (Halcrow Water/War on Want, London, 1984).

HALLIDAY, Fred and MOLYNEUX, Maxine, The Ethiopian Revolution, (Verso, London, 1981).

INTERNATIONAL INSTITUTE FOR STRATEGIC STUDIES, The Military Balance 1984-1985, (IISS, London, 1984).

JOHNSON, Michael and Trish, Eritrea: the National Question and the Logic of Protracted Struggle, (in Journal of African Affairs, May 1980).

THE LABOUR PARTY, Labour's Programme 1982, (London, 1982).

LEFORT, Rene, Ethiopia: An Heretical Revolution? (Zed Press, London, 1983).

LEONARD, Richard, Revolution and Democracy in Eritrea, (Lelio Basso Foundation, unpublished, 1983).

LEWIS, I.M. (Ed.), Nationalism and Self Determination in the Horn of Africa, (Ithaca Press, London, 1983).

MINISTRY OF INFORMATION, The First to be Freed: the Record of British Military Administration in Eritrea and Somalia, 1941-43, (His Majesty's Stationery Office, London, 1944).

MINORITY RIGHTS GROUP Report No 5, Eritrea and Tigray, Colin Legum and James Firebrace, (MRG, London, 1983).

MORCH, Henning, Analysis of Investigation into Conditions Resulting from Drought and War, (Medisinernes Eritrea Aksjon, Norway, unpublished, 1984).

NELSON, Harold and KAPLAN, Irving (Eds.), Ethiopia, a Country Study, (Area Handbook Series, Headquarters, Department of Army, Washington DC, 1981).

ORGANISATION OF AFRICAN UNITY, Charter of the Organisation of African Unity, (Addis Ababa, 1953).

---, Conference Resolutions, (Addis Ababa, 1964).

PANKHURST, E.S. Eritrea on the Eve, (Woodford Green, 1952).
PETRAS, James, The Eritrean Revolution and Contemporary World Politics, (Africa Research and Publications Project, Trenton, 1984).
POOL, David, Eritrea, Africa's Longest War, (Anti-Slavery Society, London, 1982).
Proceedings of the Permanent Peoples' Tribunal of the International League for the Rights and Liberation of People, The Eritrean Case, (Research Information Centre on Eritrea, Rome, 1982).
ROBINSON, Ian and WARDLE, Chris, Mission to Assess and Identify Agricultural Programme Possibilities in Eritrea, (Eritrea Consortium, London, unpublished, 1983).
RELIEF AND REHABILITATION COMMISSION, Assistance Requirements 1984, (Addis Ababa, March 1984).
RUBENSON, Sven, The Survival of Ethiopian Independence, (Heinemann, London, 1976).
SHERMAN, Richard, Eritrea, the Unfinished Revolution, (Praeger Publishers, New York, 1980).
SILKEN, Trish, Eritrea, (in Third World Quarterly Review, Vol V, No. 4).
SMITH, Gayle, Note on the Drought Conditions in South Western Eritrea, (unpublished report, Nov. 1983).
TEKIE FISSEHATZION, The International Dimensions of the Eritrean Question, (in Horn of Africa, vol VI, No.2).
TREVASKIS, G.K.N., Eritrea, a Colony in Transition, (Oxford University Press, London, 1960).
UNITED NATIONS, General Assembly, Final Report of the U.N. Commissioner to Eritrea, (General Assembly Official Records, VIIth Session, Supp. No. 15A/2188, 1952).
WEBBER, June, Field visit to Eritrea - Health Report, (Oxfam Canada, unpublished, 1984).

B. Magazines and Newspapers
Adulis (EPLF, Paris)
Africa Confidential (London)
Africa Economic Digest (London)
Africa Now (London)
Christian Aid News (London)
Eritrea Information (RICE, Rome)
Eritrean Medical Journal (Eritrea)
Guardian (Manchester and London)
Horn of Africa (New Jersey)
International Committee of the Red Cross Bulletin (Geneva)
Review of African Political Economy (London)
Summary of World Broadcasts (London)
War on Want News (London)
Information about the work of War on Want is available from their office at 467 Caledonian Road, London N7 9BE, England. Telephone 01 609 0211.

Authors

JAMES FIREBRACE is War on Want's programme officer for the Sahel and Horn of Africa. He previously worked as co-ordinator of the Catholic Institute for International Relations (CIIR) programme in the Yemen Arab Republic and Somalia. He is author of 'Infant Feeding in the Yemen Arab Republic' (1981), a study of the problems caused by bottle-feeding; co-author of 'The Hidden Revolution' (1982) which examines the social changes occurring in Tigray province of Ethiopia in the context of war and drought; and co-author of the 'Minority Rights Group Report on Eritrea' (1983).

STUART HOLLAND is the Labour Member of Parliament for Lambeth Vauxhall. In 1974-75 he was Special Adviser to the then Minister of Overseas Development, Rt. Hon. Judith Hart MP, and in 1983 he was appointed Shadow Minister of Overseas Development and Cooperation. His several publications include co-authorship of 'Kissinger's Kingdom? — A Counter Report on Central America', published in 1984, and 'Out of Crisis: A Project for European Recovery' (1983), which he edited for the Forum for International Political and Social Economy. Both books are published by Spokesman.

KISSINGER'S KINGDOM?

A Counter-report on Central America

Stuart Holland MP
Donald Anderson MP

Kissinger's Kingdom? results from a fact-finding mission on the initiative of Neil Kinnock, MP, Leader of the Labour Party, which the authors undertook in Central America in December 1983.

In his preface Neil Kinnock writes that "the problems of Central America are North-South, not East-West . . . the United States of America with its immense resources could change the condition of the area but only if its Governments end the historic folly of propping up dependent dictatorships and sabotaging administrations that have been produced by the crisis of under-development . . . in the USA there is an extensive body of opinion which is opposed to yet another armed crusade against some of the least privileged and most exploited people in the world, the people of Central America. They, like us, will be informed and strengthened by this report from Stuart Holland and Donald Anderson which in many important ways is a timely and necessary counter to the Kissinger Commission".

Stuart Holland, Member of Parliament for Lambeth Vauxhall, is the shadow minister for Overseas Development and Co-operation, and Donald Anderson, Member of Parliament for Swansea East, is a shadow minister for Foreign Affairs in the Parliamentary Labour Party.

£2.75   ISBN 0 85124 403 3

SPOKESMAN
Bertrand Russell House, Gamble Street, Nottingham.
Tel. 0602 708318

The Most Dangerous Decade

World militarism and the new non-aligned peace movement
by Ken Coates

In 1980, facing up to a renewed upsurge of militarism, the Bertrand Russell Peace Foundation joined forces with a number of others to launch the appeal for European Nuclear Disarmament. This began with a warning. "We are entering the most dangerous decade in history", it said. There is a good deal of new evidence to show that this appreciation was exact, containing not a milligram of exaggeration. This book looks again at the issues raised by the END Appeal, and at some of the developments since its launch, and goes on to consider the peace movement now, both within Europe and beyond it.

Paper £4.95   *ISBN 0 85124 406 8*
Cloth £15   *ISBN 0 85124 405 X*
212pp with 13 illustrations

There Are Alternatives!

Four Roads to Peace and Security
by Johan Galtung

There Are Alternatives! tells how, against all the odds, we might yet avoid a catastrophic nuclear war by initiating an alternative security policy. This would mean "transarmament" to non-provocative, non-offensive forms of defence; gradual decoupling from the superpowers; strengthening national coherence through social and political changes; and new forms of co-operation between East and West. Professor Galtung's pioneering work is inspired by the concrete politics of six European countries: Austria, Albania, Finland, Sweden, Switzerland and Yugoslavia. They constitute no threat to peace, yet have a very high level of security.

Paper £4.95   *ISBN 0 85124 394 0*
Cloth £17.50   *ISBN 0 85124 393 2*
220pp. Demy 8vo

SPOKESMAN
Bertrand Russell House, Gamble Street, Nottingham, UK
Tel. 0602 708318